Cummins, D. Duane
The origins of the Civil War

The O

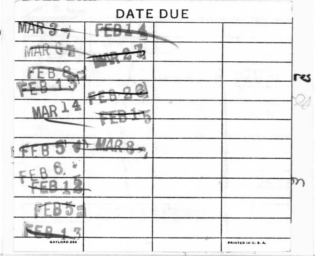

DATE DUE			
MAR 3 7	FEB 14		
MAR 6 8	MAR 23		
FEB 8			
FEB 13	FEB 28		
MAR 14	FEB 15		
FEB 5	MAR 8		
FEB 6			
FEB 12			
FEB 5			
FEB 13			

GAYLORD 234   PRINTED IN U. S. A.

Inquiries into American History

Our Colonial Heritage: Plymouth and Jamestown
by William Gee White

The Middle Colonies: New York, New Jersey, Pennsylvania
by James I. Clark

The American Revolution
by D. Duane Cummins and William Gee White

The Federal Period: 1790–1800
by Lloyd K. Musselman

Andrew Jackson's America
by Thomas Koberna and Stanley Garfinkel

The American Frontier
by D. Duane Cummins and William Gee White

The Origins of the Civil War
by D. Duane Cummins and William Gee White

Reconstruction: 1865–1877
by James I. Clark

Industrialism: The American Experience
by James E. Bruner, Jr.

American Foreign Policy: 1789–1980
by Thomas A. Fitzgerald, Jr.

Contrasting Decades: The 1920's and 1930's
by D. Duane Cummins and William Gee White

Combat and Consensus: The 1940's and 1950's
by D. Duane Cummins and William Gee White

Conflict and Compromise: The 1960's and 1970's
by D. Duane Cummins

America at War: World War I and World War II
by Douglas Waitley

America at War: Korea and Vietnam
by Douglas Waitley

Women in American History
by William Jay Jacobs

The Origins of the Civil War

D. Duane Cummins
William Gee White

Glencoe Publishing Company
Encino, California

Contributing Editor:

Dr. James I. Clark

973.6
Cu-2
11/86

REVISED EDITION

Glencoe Publishing Company
17337 Ventura Boulevard
Encino, California 91316

Collier Macmillan Canada, Ltd.

Library of Congress Catalog Card Number: 76–172056

Printed in the United States of America

ISBN 0-02-652740-5

2   3   4   5   6   7   8   90   89   88   87   86   85

For
INA Z. CUMMINS HUDSON
and
DELORES ANN CUMMINS RYAN

whose unfailing thoughtfulness and
encouragement served as a sustaining
force through many difficult years.

CONTENTS

Mourners assembled before the Lincoln home in Springfield, Illinois.

INTRODUCTION

Sir, disguise the fact as you will, there is an enmity
between the northern and southern people that is deep and
enduring, and you can never eradicate it—never! You
Republicans sit upon your side, silent and gloomy; we sit
upon ours with knit brows and portentous scowls. . . . We
are enemies as much as if we were hostile States. I believe
that the northern people hate the South worse than ever the
English people hated France; and I can tell my brethren
over there that there is no love lost upon the part of the
South.

SENATOR ALFRED IVERSON (D., Ga.),
Senate Address, December, 1860

The United States, from its earliest colonial beginnings, was
a heterogeneous society. Social life, political ideals, economic pursuits, and cultural patterns varied from colony to
colony, dictated partly by geography and partly by the
backgrounds of the people. Commerce and trade characterized the New England colonies. The middle colonies—
New York, New Jersey, Pennsylvania, and Delaware—
derived their wealth from trade and mixed agriculture. The
economy of the southern colonies rested mainly on single-
crop agriculture—tobacco, indigo, or rice. Socially, politically, and economically, the banker-commercial class dominated in the northern colonies; in the South it was the
aristocratic planter class. Differences among the sections,
however, were not strong enough to prevent a union of the
thirteen states in 1787.

9

Yet differences remained, and they rose to the surface during periods of political stress: the Alien and Sedition Acts in 1798; the War of 1812; the question of Missouri statehood in 1820; and the tariff controversy of 1832. Increasingly, congressional disputes over national policy pitted representatives from the North against those from the South. In each case, a sectional adjustment was eventually arranged and the crisis passed without serious incident. Still, bitterness grew and gradually diminished the possibility of further compromise. Despite strong ties based on a common language, as well as on the Protestant religion and English ancestry, the North and the South moved steadily apart. When the problems of California statehood and the settlement of Kansas and Nebraska appeared in the 1840's and 1850's, compromise became more difficult to achieve than ever before.

After 1857, northern and southern positions hardened, and chances of adjusting differences seemed lost. By then the generation of compromisers led by Henry Clay was dead. Few citizens of either section really wanted war, but the election of 1860, as far as many were concerned, seemed to exhaust the desire for compromise. No one appeared able to devise a formula that would preserve peace.

What could cause a reasonably prosperous and advancing nation to be torn apart by civil war? Historians have been nearly as far from agreement on this question as were the men who participated in the conflict. Did war come because Americans refused to pursue ways of compromise and accommodation used many times before 1861? Did war happen because differences between North and South were so great and so fundamental that compromise eventually became impossible? And, if so, what were those crucial differences? Were they primarily economic in nature—the agrarian South versus the commercial, industrial North? Or were they primarily political? Abraham Lincoln was elected president in 1860 without receiving a single electoral vote from a southern state. Or were they social or cultural, or perhaps a combination of all of these? Why did the separation come in 1861, when it might have occurred in 1850, 1833, 1820, or, for that matter, in 1787?

For more than a century historians have sought answers to these questions.

The Civil War, the central theme of nineteenth-century American history, has been studied more thoroughly than any other event in the nation's past. The issues and problems that emerged from the Civil War experience continue to plague Americans today: nationalism versus sectionalism and states' rights; industrialization and urbanization; the dilemma of the Negro in American society. A savage fratricidal conflict, the war was a national trauma, leaving for more than a hundred years deep feelings of guilt and resentment.

This book deals first with interpretations of the causes of the conflict. Next it considers the issues and problems that led to it and some of the men involved. Finally, it examines the battle of Gettysburg, the turning point of the war.

Abraham Lincoln, photographed by Alexander Gardner in 1863.

CHAPTER ONE

VARIATIONS

ON A THEME

... But the Government at Washington, denying our right
to self-government, refused even to listen to any proposals
for a peaceful separation. Nothing was then left to us but
to prepare for war.

JEFFERSON DAVIS, *Inaugural
Address, February 22, 1862*

... Both parties deprecated war, but one of them would
make war rather than let the nation survive, and the other
would *accept* war rather than let it perish, and the war came.

ABRAHAM LINCOLN, *Inaugural
Address, March 4, 1865*

Disagreement among scholars over the origins of the Civil
War is not surprising, for historians have argued over the
causes of every war in which this nation has participated.
Their debate over the Civil War, however, has been especially intense, and it has produced a large body of literature
on the subject. As historian Howard K. Beale noted,

Historians ... assign to the Civil War causes ranging from
one simple force or phenomenon to patterns so complex
and manifold that they include, intricately interwoven, all
the important movements, thoughts, and actions of the
decades before 1861. One writer finds in events of the
immediately preceding years an adequate explanation of the
war; another feels he must begin his story with 1831 or

even 1820; still another goes back to the importation of the first slaves, to descriptions of geographic differences before white men appeared, or to differentiation in Europe between those who settled North and South.[1]

Of all the scholars who have evaluated the various interpretations, the work of Thomas Pressly remains unexcelled. The structure of this chapter is based largely upon his scholarship.

The attack on Fort Sumter in April, 1861, narrowed the decades-long dispute between North and South. The issue now became a simple question of supporting the Union or the Confederacy. The attack forced individuals to take a stand, and attitudes among most people toward the war quickly solidified.

This was not true of all people. At the outbreak of war some southerners saw the choice between union and secession as a cruel dilemma. Robert E. Lee was one of these men. He opposed northern abolitionists; he opposed slavery; and he opposed southern extremists and the idea of secession, which he considered nothing short of revolution. Lee recognized only two governments—the United States and the state of Virginia. He was not a southern nationalist. Yet Lee had to choose, and he described the nature of his choice in an eloquent letter to his sister:

> ... The whole south is in a state of revolution, into which Virginia, after a long struggle, has been drawn; and, though I recognize no necessity for this state of things, and would have forborne and pleaded to the end for a redress of grievances, real or supposed, yet in my own person I had to meet the question whether I should take part against my native state.
>
> With all my devotion to the Union and the feeling of loyalty and duty of an American citizen, I have not been able to make up my mind to raise my hand against my relatives, my children, my home. I have therefore resigned

[1] Howard K. Beale, "What Historians Have Said About the Causes of the Civil War," in *Theory and Practice in Historical Study* (New York: Social Science Research Council, 1945), pp. 55–56.

Library of Congress

In 1852, when this portrait was made, Robert E. Lee was a superintendent at the U.S. Military Academy, West Point.

my commission in the Army, and save in defense of my native state, with the sincere hope that my poor services may never be needed, I hope I may never be called on to draw my sword. I know you will blame me; but you must think as kindly of me as you can, and believe that I have endeavored to do what I thought right.[2]

Significantly, Lee did not discuss slavery, argue the right of secession, defend the theory of states' rights, or trace complex causes back into the recesses of history. He simply said that he could not fight against his home. If necessary, he would defend it.

[2] Quoted in Douglas Southall Freeman, *Robert E. Lee: A Biography,* 4 vols. (New York: Charles Scribner's Sons, 1934), 1: 443.

Through Union Eyes

Stephen A. Douglas.

Seeking a cause for the conflict, most northern writers and politicians during the war—and for twenty years after—found it in a conspiracy of slaveowners. They pictured the North as the defender of the Union and the Constitution against unprovoked aggression by the South. Politicians proclaimed this theory throughout the North. Stephen A. Douglas, for example, announced at a Chicago gathering in 1861: "The present secession movement is the result of an enormous conspiracy formed . . . by leaders in the Southern Confederacy more than twelve months ago." According to the conspiracy theory, slaveholders were determined to rule the nation or destroy it. Aided by conspirators high in federal office, they plotted to overthrow the Constitution. Their goal was to force the nation to protect slavery in the states and the western territories. No longer able to control the government, southern politicians conspired to disrupt it.

Northern writers placed war guilt squarely on the South. By assaulting the nation, they said, the Confederates had attacked the principles of representative government. Therefore, they were traitors. Secession, these writers insisted, was synonymous with rebellion. They were careful, however, not to blame all the people of the seceded states, but only a small group of southern conspirators. Henry Wilson, Massachusetts senator from 1855 to 1873 and United States vice-president under Ulysses S. Grant, wrote *A History of the Rise and Fall of the Slave Power in America.* This work, published between 1872 and 1877, typified northern attitudes of the time. The "slave power," said Wilson,

> . . . after aggressive warfare of more than two generations upon the vital and animating spirit of republican institutions, upon the cherished and hallowed sentiments of a Christian people, upon the enduring interests and lasting renown of the Republic, organized treasonable conspiracies, raised the standard of revolution, and plunged the nation into a bloody contest for the preservation of its threatened life.[3]

[3] Quoted in Thomas Pressly, *Americans Interpret Their Civil War* (Princeton: Princeton University Press, 1961), p. 39.

THE HURLY-BURLY POT.

An 1850 cartoon deploring the personalities and issues that seemed destined to rip the union apart. The cartoonist compares David Wilmot, William Lloyd Garrison, John Calhoun, and Horace Greeley with the witches in *Macbeth*.

Union writers like Wilson were advocates of a cause. They wrote not long after a time when men were dying on the battlefield, and it is not surprising that they reflected wartime passions. Neither is it surprising that they expressed themselves in moralistic terms. Most people when seeking to justify wartime behavior tend to emphasize the righteousness of their position and the evil of their opponents'.

The Confederate View

The conspiracy theory, of course, had a double edge. It was not a northern monopoly. Southerners agreed that the deliberate actions of a small group of wicked men had led to war. But all those men lived above the Mason-Dixon line. They included "Black Republicans," abolitionists, and other northern extremists who were willing to destroy the

Union and the Constitution in order to enhance the power of the North and the Republican party.

During the war years and after, southern writers painted lurid pictures of an aggressive North bent on destroying the South and its institutions. Chief among the offenders were the abolitionists. These creatures, southerners said, had been determined to provoke slave insurrections as well as encourage blacks to escape. At the same time, the domineering North had ruthlessly exploited the South, using unconstitutional means in an effort to gain political and economic control of the nation, while southerners had resisted tyranny and defended the right of self-government.

Southerners insisted that the war was not a moral conflict over slavery. The prohibition of slavery in northern states had nothing to do with morality or humanitarianism. It was based solely on the fact that northern soil and climate were unsuited to slavery. The institution, they said, was only the occasion, or the excuse, for conflict.

The term "Civil War" found no favor in the South. Nor did the "War of the Rebellion." Both implied southern guilt. Southerners preferred to call it the "War Between the States," or the "War for Southern Independence," both of which seemed to justify their emphasis on states' rights.

The most popular of the southern writers during the immediate postwar period was Edward A. Pollard. He called the secession movement a "revolution," but he carefully emphasized its conservative character and purpose. The South, in Pollard's view, sought not to destroy existing institutions, but to preserve them. It waged a war for independence, not a crusade for new social experiments. The South seceded only to escape northern oppression. The Union by 1860 no longer afforded southerners security and protection; their institutions and their property were threatened by northern fanaticism.

The Needless War

While northern and southern partisans attacked each other as conspirators, a third group of writers and politicians developed another theory. Its origin lay among peace advocates in both North and South, a minority of men who be-

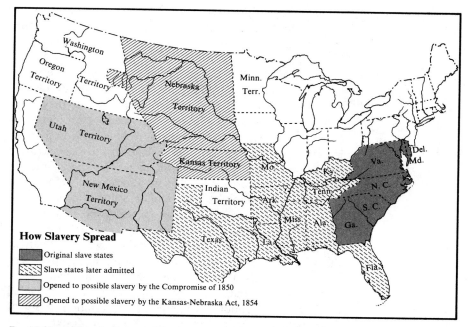

How Slavery Spread

- Original slave states
- Slave states later admitted
- Opened to possible slavery by the Compromise of 1850
- Opened to possible slavery by the Kansas-Nebraska Act, 1854

By 1860, slavery had spread far beyond the borders of the six original slave states and seemed likely to spread still farther.

lieved that the war need not have taken place. The rantings and uncompromising attitudes of extremists on both sides had brought it on, they said.

These men maintained that there was no substantive issue important enough in 1861 to justify the use of arms. The struggle emerged from artificial disputes created by the agitations of abolitionist and secessionist demagogues. The conflict was pictured as a struggle between two evil principles—abolitionism and secessionism.

In the early 1860's advocates of the needless war theory unsuccessfully lobbied for immediate cessation of the conflict. However, neither during the war or immediately thereafter did the "needless" interpretation of the causes and nature of the war find much favor.

The Irrepressible Conflict

A quarter of a century after Appomattox the war had become history. Union troops had long since withdrawn from the South; blue and gray veterans now held occasional joint reunions. Passions had cooled. The South had been welcomed back into the Union.

In the late 1890's the people of the United States were becoming increasingly interested in affairs and events beyond the borders of the country. This interest may have served partly as a distraction from internal problems—a severe depression at the beginning of the decade and growing farm and labor unrest—but, whatever the reasons, there was a new spirit of nationalism in the air, and America would soon fight a war with Spain and acquire colonies.

A new generation of historians had come of age. Most of them had been mere boys in the 1860's, and their memories of the war were fragmented and dim, free from the emotionalism that characterized those who wrote about the war as it progressed and soon after it ended. These historians' views reflected the spirit of nationalism felt throughout the country. They formed what has been called the nationalist school of Civil War interpretation. A list of them includes James Ford Rhodes, John McMaster, Albert Bushnell Hart, Edward Channing, Woodrow Wilson, and William A. Dunning.

Nationalist historians placed great emphasis on the term "Civil War," for the conflict, they said, resulted from a struggle between rival nationalisms, conflicting social orders, and differing economic systems—between impersonal, complex forces. In their view, economic, social, and political differences between North and South were so great that war was inevitable; it was an "irrepressible" conflict.

This idea was first advanced in a speech given by the Republican politician William H. Seward in Rochester, New York, in October, 1858. Seward entitled his address "The Irrepressible Conflict," and in it called the country "a theater, which exhibits, in full operation, two radically different political systems; the one resting on the basis of servile or slave labor, the other on the basis of voluntary labor of freemen." The two systems, Seward believed, could not exist peacefully in one country. Abraham Lincoln expressed much the same idea in his "A House Divided" speech five months earlier at the state Republican convention in Springfield, Illinois. In that address Lincoln warned,

> A house divided against itself cannot stand. I believe this government cannot endure, permanently half *slave* and half *free*. I do not expect the Union to be *dissolved*—I do not expect the house to *fall*—but I *do* expect it will cease to be divided. It will become *all* one thing, or *all* the other.

Abraham Lincoln.

One of the first works in the nationalist tradition, and in some respects the most influential, was that by James Ford Rhodes. His *History of the United States from the Compromise of 1850 to the McKinley-Bryan Campaign of 1896* was published in several volumes between 1893 and 1920. These books established Rhodes as a leading historian, and scholars and ordinary citizens alike praised him for his impartial treatment of the issues leading to the Civil War. According to Rhodes, slavery lay at the heart of the sectional dispute. It was the main cause of war. Yet Rhodes distinguished between the moral and political aspects of slavery; he declared that differences in ways of life between North and South were so vast that political compromise in 1860 could have done little more than delay a war that was inevitable. He did not attempt to place personal or sectional guilt for the war on southerners or the South. Nor did he blame southerners for slavery. He found much to admire about the Old South, and placed responsibility for the institution of slavery on inanimate forces, suggesting that cotton and the cotton gin had fostered it and made it profitable.

Other nationalist historians followed Rhodes' lead. They too stressed deep sectional differences as the cause of war. According to Edward Channing, for example,

> By the middle of the century, two distinct social organizations had developed within the United States, the one in the South and the other in the North. Southern society was based on the production of staple agricultural crops by slave labor. Northern society was bottomed on varied employments—agricultural, mechanical, and commercial—all carried on under the wage system.

Bureau of Engraving and Printing

"After the Wedding in Warren, Pennsylvania," by an unknown artist, 1862.

Two such divergent forms of society could not continue
indefinitely to live side by side within the walls of one
government. . . . One or the other of these societies
must perish, or both must secure complete equality, . . .
or the two societies must separate absolutely and live
each by itself under its own government. . . .[4]

Frederick Jackson Turner, mainly concerned with the
influence of the frontier on American history, tended to reinforce the sectional and irrepressible conflict theory. Turner, however, thought Rhodes and others had overlooked
one important section—the West. Turner believed that
the addition of a third dimension to the study of Civil
War causes was crucial. Had there not been new lands to
settle in the West, said Turner, the question of the extension of slavery would not have arisen. The acquisition of

[4] Edward Channing, *A History of the United States*, 6 vols.
(New York: Macmillan Co., 1907–1925), 6: 3–4.

"Home on the Mississippi River," by an unknown artist, painted about 1865.

new lands and the aggressive spread of the institution, he suggested, forced people to make moral judgments about it.

The irrepressible conflict theory continued to enjoy popularity well into the twentieth century. Arthur C. Cole published one of the more influential books on the theory in 1934. In *The Irrepressible Conflict,* he noted the differences between North and South that led to war in these somewhat figurative words:

> . . . The spirit of democracy and the cause of free land spread their influence over the industrial North. The railroad pushed its iron bands across the country binding together the young commonwealths and the old. The fruits of a new and glowing prosperity were tasted in the great agricultural empire as well as in the Eastern marts of trade and manufacture. The throbbing forces of enlightenment, culture and humanitarian reform spread over the North, while free labor, girding its loins, began to feel its power.

South of the Ohio's murky waters a plantation oligarchy basked contentedly in the waning sun of prosperity. For the few, life was easy and pleasant; culture—measured in terms of passive leisure-class enjoyment and not in science and the creative arts—was within ready reach. An army of Negro vassals and a dependent white class made obeisance to planter rule, though the white yeomanry stirred restlessly as its opportunities of rising to a share in the plantation regime steadily declined and slave labor threatened to become a fatal incubus upon the back of Dixie.[5]

The Second American Revolution

By the time Cole wrote *The Irrepressible Conflict,* another group of historians—the progressives—had made their contribution to an understanding of the war. These men achieved maturity during the Progressive Era (1890–1914) when magazine writers, university professors, social workers, and others were focusing attention on problems related to poverty and squalor in the cities, huge monopolistic corporations, industrialization and urbanization, and the development of labor unions. The progressives interpreted American history in terms of conflicts between classes, between the haves and the have-nots of society. They were more concerned with the problems of economic democracy than with those of political democracy.

Charles A. Beard was foremost among the progressive historians. In his *Rise of American Civilization,* published in 1927, he called the Civil War the "Second American Revolution." The first, said Beard, had been a political revolution, during which the Americans had won independence from Britain. The second was economic, enabling northern industrialism to triumph over southern agrarianism and changing the nation's course profoundly.

Beard described the Civil War as a social and economic conflict that ended with the unquestioned establishment of a new power in control of the federal government. The war brought vast changes in the arrangement of social classes,

[5] Arthur Charles Cole, *The Irrepressible Conflict, 1850–1865* (New York: Macmillan Co., 1934), pp. 406–407. Copyright 1934 by Macmillan Publishing Co., Inc., renewed 1962 by Arthur Charles Cole.

in industrial development, and in the accumulation and distribution of wealth.

According to Beard, the real struggle between the North and the South was over which section would control the federal government to its own economic and political advantage. The nation had changed since its formation in 1789. A dynamic, entrepreneurial, industrial capitalism had risen in the North. Pitted against it for control of the government was a static, aristocratic, agrarian plantation society in the South. The South, wanting low-priced manufactured goods, opposed high tariffs; in 1832 South Carolina had threatened to leave the Union over the tariff issue. The North, to protect and further industrialization and expand its markets, favored high tariffs, which would decrease competition from foreign goods. The North endorsed laws that were favorable to banks and those that provided federal aid to railroads and industries. The South generally opposed these measures because that section benefited little from them. The North was against slavery in the western states and territories because its leaders saw economic and political advantage in leaving those areas open to settlement by farmers and members of the working classes. The South, in order to protect its influence in the federal government, wanted a balance maintained between free and slave states as the Union expanded westward. The South also insisted on a strong fugitive slave law as a means of protecting its economic interests.

Slavery, according to Beard and other progressives, was not a strong moral issue anywhere. Southerners needed slavery to support their agriculture. Northerners did not; and, except for the abolitionists, they opposed it only in the territories, not in the South itself.

Until 1860, the South had generally controlled the national government. Tariffs were kept low and a homestead act that would have made western settlement easier was vetoed by the president, James Buchanan. The Kansas-Nebraska Act of 1854, which permitted the voters of those territories to decide for themselves whether or not they wanted slavery, was favorable to the South, as was the Dred Scott decision of 1857, in which the Supreme

Missouri Historical Society

Dred Scott. In 1857, the U.S. Supreme Court ruled that he was not a citizen or even a person, but rather was property.

Court ruled that persons who had been slaves, or whose ancestors had been slaves, did not have the rights of free citizens, and that Congress did not have the power to ban slavery in the territories. But the election of Abraham Lincoln in 1860 threatened Southern control. With Republicans in power, northern businessmen and industrialists could get what they wanted—federal grants to build a transcontinental railroad, high tariffs, and a homestead act. These changes might not come about as soon as the Republicans took office in 1861, but they would come at some time in the future. To most southern politicians, the handwriting on the wall was clear.

Nationalist historians had considered the results of the war good because the sections had been forced to continue as one nation. Although Beardian scholars did not question the value of unity, they nonetheless condemned the consequences of the war. It ended, they said, with the economy dominated by capitalists who were guided almost exclusively by their appetites for profit. This led inevitably to corporation control of government, monopoly, the exploitation of labor and farmers, and a severe depletion of natural resources.

Beard and other progressives agreed with the nationalists on one thing: the war had been inevitable. But the war, they said, was only a fleeting incident in the larger social and economic story. The Second American Revolution, economic in nature, marked the dividing line between the agricultural and the industrial era in the United States.

New Southern Voices

In the 1930's southern historians raised their voices once again. Unlike their predecessors of the immediate postwar period, they did not stress the conspiracy theory, but they did place the blame for the war on the North and they did defend the southern way of life. Among this group of historians were Ulrich B. Phillips, Charles W. Ramsdell, and Frank L. Owsley.

These scholars portrayed the antebellum southern culture as far better and more desirable than the urbanized and industrial way of life which resulted from the North's victory. They tended to idealize the Old South and its institutions while describing the North in hostile, deprecating terms.

According to Frank Owsley, the basic cause of the Civil War was the "egocentric nationalism" of the North. He accused the North of having thought of *itself* as the nation, seeking to destroy the sectional balance of power and failing to recognize the dignity and legitimate concerns of people in other sections. Owsley was especially critical of northern abolitionists who, he said, harped unremittingly on false issues to arouse public opinion against the South. He denied that slavery was a cause of the war. In essence,

An early steel plant in Cincinnati, Ohio, 1832. Cincinnati was the gateway to the frontier, and for years the largest inland city in the United States.

Owsley combined the Beardian interpretation with some of the attitudes of southern writers of the 1860's and 1870's.

Ulrich B. Phillips emphasized the race factor. The great physical differences between the white and black races, he said, coupled with the divergent social and cultural levels of the two groups, were fundamental to an explanation of the plantation-slavery system. Phillips concluded that the primary function of the system had been the schooling and civilizing of the Negro race. He further insisted that the best interests of both races had required the maintenance of a system of racial adjustment controlled by whites. He characterized Negroes as ignorant and naturally lazy, but he believed that the plantation system had trained this "savage race" to a degree of fitness for life in the white community. Benefits had outweighed disadvantages but, unfortunately, the whole plantation way of life had been destroyed by the war. Phillips considered northern abolitionists and their agitation against the southern system the major cause of the war.

Phillips' interpretation, like Owsley's, was reminiscent of

The New York Public Library

Slaves enjoying themselves after the annual hog-butchering. This picture comes from a book that was designed to "answer" *Uncle Tom's Cabin.*

the attitudes of southerners of the preceding century. In addition, both held the same opinion on the necessity of a system for racial discipline.

The Repressible Conflict

During the 1930's still another group of historians took a look at the evidence and produced a new interpretation of the Civil War period. These men, members of the revisionist school, stood the irrepressible conflict theory on its head. The war, they said, could have been avoided if men of the time had not been swayed by passion and propaganda and instead had chosen to find a way to compromise sectional differences. It was, revisionists said, a needless and tragic war.

At the time Avery O. Craven, James G. Randall, and other revisionist historians wrote, Americans and Europeans alike felt a deep revulsion toward war. They retained vivid memories of World War I. That holocaust, many

Americans were convinced, had been needless; they believed that war as a means of solving problems was barbaric, criminal, and unnecessary. The revisionist interpretation of Civil War causes was well received.

Craven argued that the economic, social, and political differences between North and South could not account for the war. After all, a number of nations with pronounced dissimilarities of land and people within their borders had never resorted to civil war. Nor would Craven accept slavery as a cause for war. He blamed abolitionists for blowing up the issue out of all proportion to its importance, propagandizing it until passions rose to such a peak that positions on the question polarized. Craven assumed that the nonviolent abolition of slavery would have been possible through internal reform, if the issue had not been so emotionalized that it could no longer be dealt with in rational terms.

Abolitionists alone were not at fault, said Craven. He blamed extremists northern *and* southern. "Stripped of false assumptions," he wrote,

> the tragedy of the nation in bloody strife from 1861 to 1865 must, in large part, be charged to a generation of well-meaning Americans, who, busy with the task of getting ahead, permitted their short-sighted politicians, their over-zealous editors, and their pious reformers to emotionalize real and potential differences and to conjure up distorted impressions of those who dwelt in other parts of the nation. For more than two decades, these molders of public opinion steadily created the fiction of two distinct peoples contending for the right to preserve and expand their sacred cultures. . . . They awakened new fears and led men to hate. . . .[6]

James G. Randall believed that no issue was so vital as to require a violent solution. He agreed with Craven that the responsibility for the Civil War must be placed on a "blundering generation," the men of the 1850's and the

---

[6] Avery O. Craven, *The Coming of the Civil War* (Chicago: University of Chicago Press, 1950), p. 2.

1860's in both the North and the South. In this respect the repressible conflict theory is similar to the needless war theory advanced by one group of Civil War contemporaries. Emotionalism, irresponsible politicians, and propaganda brought on a war that could and should have been avoided.

Recent Points of View

Since the revisionists wrote, there have been no new interpretations of why war came. One distinguished recent work on the causes of the Civil War, Allan Nevins' *The Ordeal of the Union,* seems to blend the irrepressible and repressible theories along with a touch of Ulrich Phillips. Nevins suggests that war could have been avoided, and he is highly critical of the leadership of presidents Zachary Taylor, Franklin Pierce, and James Buchanan during the 1850's. On the other hand, Nevins asserts that the question of slavery was irrepressible and could not be compromised. One section had to yield its fundamental position. He comes close to Phillips in stating that slavery was primarily a problem of racial adjustment, and he considers it the main cause of the war.

James Buchanan.

Writing in 1949, Arthur Schlesinger, Jr., took issue with revisionist historians. None of them, he noted, identified policies that contemporary figures might have adopted instead of war. He posed the question: If the war could have been avoided, what course should American leaders have followed with respect to slavery?

Schlesinger listed three alternatives: (1) the South might have abolished slavery by itself if left alone; (2) slavery would have died because it was economically unsound; (3) the North might have offered some form of compensated emancipation. He then proceeded to demolish each of these alternatives as either inadequate or unattainable. Schlesinger pointed out that southern liberals had not been able to end slavery in any one of the states. Did that reveal anything about the possibility of reform?

The war was fought over the moral issue of slavery and the future of the Negro in America, Schlesinger said. And he criticized revisionists for failing to make a moral judgment on the question. The South, Schlesinger argued, was a closed society, granting individual rights and freedoms only to whites. To ask northerners not to disapprove of this, he stated, was like saying that there should have been no anti-Nazis during the 1930's. The moral issue of slavery was too profound to be solved by political compromise.

It is interesting to note that Schlesinger's generation had lived through World War II, a bloody cataclysm in which the issues of right and wrong had seemed very sharply drawn: the aggressive, fascist Axis powers against the peace-loving, democratic Allied powers. The Nazis' racial policy, the full horror of which was not revealed to the rest of the world until the end of the war, was difficult even to contemplate. That such a policy might have been compromised over, or accommodated in any country in western Europe, was unthinkable. Furthermore, the Cold War was just settling in, splitting the world into two seemingly irreconcilable camps: the Communist world against the Free world. It is not surprising that Schlesinger wrote and thought in terms of irrepressible conflict, or that historical interpretation had come full circle, back to the nationalist emphasis of James Ford Rhodes and Edward Channing.

The Problems Today

Although interpretations of the causes of the Civil War had come full circle by the 1950's, the extremely complex question of why war came was far from settled. Students today must cope with the same problems that have confronted historians for over a century. Was slavery simply an excuse used by the North to establish domination over the South, or was the moral issue of slavery the real reason for the war? What role did social, economic, and political differences play in the war's coming? Was the war a repressible or an irrepressible conflict? Did American leaders fail?

The issues of the 1850's and 1860's are with Americans today. And as long as historians investigate the role of the Negro in American society, debate the wisdom of fighting wars, and study majority rule and minority rights, the causes of the Civil War will remain a matter of dispute.

SUGGESTED READINGS

Craven, Avery O. *The Coming of the Civil War*. University of Chicago Press, Phoenix Books.

Craven, Avery O. *The Historian and the Civil War*. University of Chicago Press, Phoenix Books.

Phillips, Ulrich B. *The Course of the South to Secession: An Interpretation*. Edited by E. M. Coulter. Hill & Wang, American Century Series.

Pressly, Thomas. *Americans Interpret Their Civil War*. Free Press.

Rhodes, James Ford. *History of the United States from the Compromise of 1850*. Edited by Allan Nevins. University of Chicago Press, Phoenix Books.

Rozwenc, Edwin. *The Causes of the American Civil War*. D. C. Heath.

Stampp, Kenneth, ed. *The Causes of the Civil War*. Prentice-Hall, Spectrum Books.

An 1837 advertisement—known as a "broadside"—offering land for sale in the western part of New York State. This land was bought by New York City speculators, who hoped to resell it in smaller lots at a higher price. Overspeculation in land contributed to the panic and depression of 1837.

CHAPTER TWO

THE DEVELOPMENT

OF SECTIONAL

CONFLICT

"Nothing is more striking to a European traveler in the United States," observed Alexis de Tocqueville in the 1830's, "than the absence of what we term the Government, or the Administration." Having come to America in 1831 to see how its democracy worked, the young French aristocrat was impressed by the federal government's apparent lack of influence on the people. De Tocqueville probably could not have made such an observation a few years earlier, but he visited the United States on the eve of great social and political change. The brief period of nationalistic fervor and apparent national unity following the War of 1812 had subsided. Now, as the nation continued to expand, sectional attitudes were becoming more pronounced.

Almost all the thirteen million citizens of the United States in 1830 lived between the Atlantic Ocean and the Mississippi River. A few pockets of wilderness remained in that area, some still inhabited by Indians, but these would soon be settled. Beyond the Mississippi were areas of prairies, plains, mountains, and deserts. Part of this region belonged to the United States through the Louisiana Purchase; the southwestern part of the present nation was claimed by Mexico and part of the northwestern portion by England.

The United States was a rural nation in 1830. Only one in twenty Americans lived in a city of more than 8,000 inhabitants, and New York was the country's largest city with a population of about 200,000. About six million people lived in New England and the Middle Atlantic states, while the population of the southern states probably numbered fewer than five million, including blacks. The land north of the Ohio River, along with Tennessee and Kentucky, held two to three million people. A few thousand Americans lived west of the Mississippi, principally in Arkansas, Missouri, and Louisiana.

By 1830 three distinct sections of the nation had emerged: the South, the North, and the West. Each was influenced by its own particular geography and identified by its own political and social institutions. Each was represented in Congress by sectionally oriented spokesmen who reflected the views and aspirations of their constituents on such issues as tariffs, internal improvements, and territorial expansion.

Andrew Jackson was president at the time de Tocqueville toured the United States. Although a westerner, Jackson was an ardent nationalist. His southern vice-president, John C. Calhoun of South Carolina, by 1831 had become something else. In an address he gave that year he openly expressed the southern sectional view of the Constitution and the Union. Said Calhoun:

> The great and leading principle is, that the General Government emanated from the people of the several States, forming distinct political communities, and acting in their separate and sovereign capacity, and not from all of the people forming one aggregate political community; that the Constitution of the United States is, in fact, a compact, to which each State is a party. . . .

Early in his political career Calhoun had been a leading advocate of nationalism. Along with Henry Clay and other southern and western "War Hawks," he had successfully demanded war in 1812 against Great Britain for outrages

Culver Pictures

Andrew Jackson, president from 1829 to 1837.

against American national honor. Daniel Webster, who would later be the great spokesman for national unity, opposed the War of 1812, as did most of his fellow New Englanders. The careers of such men as Calhoun and Webster reflected the changes that had occurred in sectional attitudes by 1830.

Land of Industry and Commerce

In the 1830's, the section of the country generally referred to as the North included New England and the Middle Atlantic states of New York, New Jersey, and Pennsylvania. New England was, and is, made up of the six northeastern states of Massachusetts, Connecticut, Rhode Island, New Hampshire, Vermont, and Maine.

American Stock Photos

The city of Boston, seen from the harbor, in 1850.

The first New England settlements had developed around Massachusetts and Narragansett bays. The difficulty of farming the thin, rocky soil characteristic of much of New England, together with the abundance of good harbors, led many New Englanders to careers associated with the sea. Boston, the hub of New England, was an important center of commerce and culture by 1830. Hides and tallow came there from California, along with furs from the Oregon country, minerals and manufactured goods from Europe, and cotton from the South.

America's factory system began in New England, where there were numerous rivers and streams to provide the water power on which the early mills depended, and where a stable, prosperous commercial economy meant that capital and credit were readily available to finance industrializa-

The first cotton gin, in use by 1794, made it possible for one man to process over fifty pounds of cotton a day.

tion. The South also had water power, but it lacked the capital necessary to stimulate industrial growth; its money was tied up in land and slaves.

The first cotton thread spun by machine in America was produced by Samuel Slater and Moses Brown in their textile factory at Pawtucket, Rhode Island, in 1791. Slater, an English immigrant who had worked with James Hargreaves, inventor of the spinning jenny, left England with plans for complicated textile machinery in his head. Working from memory, he built the machines that he and Brown lodged in their mill.

Two years later, a New Englander named Eli Whitney completed an invention that would profoundly affect both the industrial economy of the North and the agricultural economy of the South: the cotton gin. In 1798, at his gun factory in New Haven, Connecticut, Whitney developed another technological innovation that would have far-reaching consequences for American industry: the concept of standardized, interchangeable parts. Before that time, guns and other complex mechanisms had been made individually by skilled craftsmen. The process was time-consuming, and the size and shape of the various parts differed

The Boott Cotton Mills in Lowell, Massachusetts, 1852. The mill owners provided a park for their employees.

from gun to gun, making repairs costly. By inventing machines to turn out identical, interchangeable parts, Whitney opened the way for the techniques of mass assembly and mass production.

Samuel Slater had violated English laws prohibiting the export of machines or information about them when he smuggled the design for a spinning machine out of England by memorizing the blueprints. In 1812, Francis Cabot Lowell also broke those laws to bring to America the design for a power loom. Lowell built a textile factory at Waltham, Massachusetts, where, for the first time, the entire process of producing cloth, from spinning to weaving, was done as part of the same operation. Lowell later established cotton mills on the Merrimack River, the town that grew up around them being named after him.

Young people, who found little to keep them on the small, poor farms of New England, were attracted to the mills, factories, and business houses of Boston, Providence, New Haven, and other New England cities. Harriett Martineau, who traveled extensively in New England during the 1830's and wrote a book about her experiences, described the factories she visited in Waltham. Much of the human labor in the cotton mills was supplied by children and young girls, about whom Miss Martineau wrote:

> The girls earn two, and some three, dollars a week, besides
> their board. The little children earn one dollar a week.
> Most of the girls live in the houses provided by the corpora-
> tion, which accommodate from six to eight each. When
> sisters come to the mill, it is a common practice for them to
> bring their mother to keep house for them and some of their
> companions in a dwelling built by their own earnings. In
> this case, they save enough out of their board to clothe
> themselves, and have their two or three dollars a week to
> spare. Some have thus cleared off mortgages from their
> fathers' farms; others have educated the hope of the family
> at college; and many are rapidly accumulating an inde-
> pendence. I saw a whole street of houses built with the
> earnings of the girls; some with piazzas, and green venetian
> blinds; and all neat and sufficiently spacious.[1]

The town of Lowell was an attraction for any visitor.
Visitors invariably contrasted Lowell with textile towns in
England, where underpaid factory workers led a life of
hopelessness. William T. Thompson, a Georgia planter and
newspaper editor who visited Lowell in 1845, wrote: "It
was indeed a interestin sight, and a gratifyin one to a person who has always thought that the opparatives as they
call 'em in the Northern factories, was the most miserable
kind of people in the world."

> We tuck a stroll on the banks of the Merrymack, below
> the town. From different pints we got a fine view of the
> place. We was passin up Merrymack street to our hotel
> when the bells rung, and the fust thing we know'd the
> whole town was full of galls. They cum swarmin out of the
> factories like bees out of a hive, and spreadin in evry direc-
> tion, filled the streets so that nothin else was to be seen
> but platoons of sun bonnets, with long capes hangin down
> over the shoulders of the factory galls. Thousands upon
> thousands of 'em was passin along the streets, all lookin as

[1] Quoted in Warren S. Tryon, ed., *My Native Land: Life in
America, 1790–1870* (Chicago: University of Chicago Press,
1952), pp. 111–112.

happy, and cheerful, and neat, and clean, and butiful, as if they was boardin-school misses jest from ther books.

The next mornin the sun was jest up when we went down on to the corporashuns, as they call 'em here, whar the mills are. It was a most lovely mornin. The factorys was all still. The yards in frunt of the bildins was clean, and the little flower-gardens by the dores was glitterin with due. . . . Ther wasn't many peeple to be seed in the streets. Now and then we could see sum men gwine to the countin-rooms and offices, or to the factorys, but the cracker-bonnets was in eclipse. The galls was at breckfust at their boardin-houses, which are neat two, and sumtimes three story brick houses, what stand in blocks near the factorys, and is owned by the proprietors of the mills.

Bimeby the bells rung. In a minit more the streets leading to the mills was swarmin with galls. Here they cum in evry direction, laughin and talkin to one another in groops and pairs, or singly, all lookin as merry and happy as if they was gwine to a frollic, insted of to ther work.

They poured into the mills by thousands, like bees into a hive, and in a few minits more the noise of the machinery begun to git louder and louder, until each factory sent out a buzzin sound, with which all other sounds soon becum mixed up, until it seemed we was into a city whar men, wimmin and children, water, fire, and light, was all at work, and whar the very air breathed the song of industry.[2]

There was, of course, another side to factory life. Regulations required employees to work in the same room from sunrise to sunset six days a week. They could not leave the factory without permission of the overseer. They were responsible for any damage to the machines and they had to make up all lost time before they were paid. Unnecessary conversation was taboo, as were reading, eating, or smoking in the mill. Employers allowed their hired hands twenty-five minutes each for breakfast and supper and thirty min-

[2] Quoted in J. C. Furnas, *The Americans: A Social History of the United States* (New York: G. P. Putnam's Sons, 1969), p. 550. Copyright © 1969 by J. C. Furnas. Reprinted by permission of G. P. Putnam's Sons.

utes for the midday meal. They required either four weeks' notice of intention to leave or the forfeiture of four weeks' pay.

Still, at least during the early years, factory jobs were not oppressive for New England farm girls. Few of those who labored in the mills intended to work seventy hours a week for the remainder of their lives. They stayed but a few years, saving $300 to $400 to begin married life or to pay tuition at a female academy and prepare to be teachers back home or in the West.

At this time the departure of rural New Englanders for city factories and mills was matched by the loss of rural population to western states and territories. As a region, New England was the prime contributor to the expansion of the frontier and the development of the West. Traditional New England attributes of individualism, belief in the rewards of hard work, and sense of community responsibility were carried by descendants of the Puritans to such new states as Illinois and Indiana and beyond to the Far West.

Yankee trading ships were responsible for inspiring American interest in California. In the 1830's, Nathaniel J. Wyeth, intent upon securing a fortune in the western fur trade, led New England missionaries to the Oregon Country, opening a transcontinental route to the Pacific Northwest. Wyeth, in the words of historian Bernard De Voto, was "a typical Yankee business man of the period, a type which had spread American commerce all over the world . . . and who possessed enterprise, ingenuity, versatility in innovation, guts, and willingness to run risks for a profit."[3]

Another New Englander, John Bidwell, led the first emigrant train to California, while Oregon-bound pioneers were greeted by Marcus and Narcissa Whitman—New England missionaries—at their Washington mission in Walla Walla. Yankee leadership in the Far West was exemplified by such trappers and traders as Jedediah Smith and the Bent brothers, and by such colonizers as Brigham Young.

During the thirty years prior to 1820, some 800,000

[3] Bernard De Voto, *Across the Wide Missouri* (Boston: Houghton Mifflin, 1964), p. 61. Used with permission of the publisher.

The junction of the Erie Canal, which stretched 363 miles across New York from the Hudson River at Albany to Lake Erie at Buffalo, and the Northern Canal, which led to Lake Champlain and northern New England, about 1830.

New Englanders migrated west, a number equivalent to more than one-third the total population of that section of the nation. This loss of people, principally to the rich and unoccupied lands north of the Ohio, increased after the Erie Canal opened in 1825 and again after steamboats began to ply the Great Lakes in the 1830's. During the 1840's railroads were built to connect Boston and the port cities of the Great Lakes. This facilitated the migration of young people out of New England, and it also brought to the region a flood of cheap agricultural produce. New England farmers began to suffer from this western competition.

New England factory and mill owners were also faced with competition. Because they were bigger and their volume of production was greater, British mills could produce cotton cloth more cheaply than those in New England, even though both secured their raw cotton from the American South. British factory owners also paid lower wages. New England textile manufacturers were forced to pay higher wages because the labor supply was initially smaller than in Great Britain. This labor shortage helps to account

Museum of the City of New York

Irish immigrants arriving at The Battery in New York City, about 1855.

for New England's opposition to westward expansion, which lured away potential factory workers. It also influenced the region's insistence on high tariffs on manufactured goods in order to protect local factories from foreign competition.

New England in 1830 had a population of about two million, and over the next twenty years that number grew by only 700,000. Much of this relatively small gain was due to foreign immigration, some three-fourths of which came from Ireland.

Dependent on the potato as a staple in their diet, the Irish were hard-hit during the 1840's when plant diseases caused crop failures and brought on famine. In 1847 alone, more than 37,000 starving Irish immigrants landed at Boston, presenting an enormous problem to that city of 120,000. Had these immigrants been of the same sturdy Irish stock that earlier had helped to build New England's roads and canals, employers probably would have welcomed them. Many of these destitute and starving people, however, were incapable of performing much hard labor. Some, women especially, took work at low wages in textile mills, enabling employers to reduce labor costs. Eventually, foreign-born workers replaced New England farm girls in most of the mills.

Alarmed at the numbers and physical condition of the Irish immigrants, Boston authorities required all incoming ships to submit to inspection, and quarantined any ship carrying persons ill with contagious diseases. These hordes of Irish, it was declared, were making Massachusetts "the moral cess pool of the civilized world." Cecil Woodham-Smith summarized the attitude of Boston natives toward this great minority group:

> By a curious piece of reasoning, the Irish starving in Ireland were regarded as unfortunate victims, to be generously helped, while the same Irish, having crossed the Atlantic to starve in Boston, were described as the scourings of Europe and resented as an intolerable burden to the taxpayer.[4]

Not until 1850 was an effective immigrant society established in Boston to assist newly arrived immigrants.

Anti-Catholic agitation, aimed principally at the Irish, was strong during the 1830's and 1840's in New England. There were riots and demonstrations and during one incident a convent was burned.

In contrast to those who were so uncharitable toward Irish immigrants, many New Englanders demonstrated a strong humanitarian spirit and an active interest in social reform. It was in Boston in 1831 that William Lloyd Garrison announced his determination to battle slavery to the death, to abolish the institution in America. As secretary of the Massachusetts State Board of Education, Horace Mann campaigned for the extension of free public education and better training for teachers. Dorothea Dix traveled in New England and other regions in the 1840's, inspecting jails and prisons and arousing the public to compel legislators to reform their penal systems and establish separate institutions for the mentally ill, hitherto lodged in jails and treated as hopeless lunatics. Hundreds of New England

---

[4] Cecil Woodham-Smith, *The Great Hunger* (New York: Harper & Row, 1962), p. 247.

A cartoon satirizing the numerous causes and fads of the 1850's.

women lobbied to outlaw the sale of liquor, hoping by its prohibition to improve the lot of the poor. These early prohibitionists reasoned that workers must be protected from the temptation of alcohol, which caused them to spend their hard-earned pay foolishly and to neglect their families. And New England women were well represented at the first national convention for women's rights at Seneca Falls, New York, in 1848. Women wanted better educational opportunities, the right to own property in their own names, and eventually the right to vote.

As early as the 1820's, Mrs. Anne Royall, visiting the region, noted New England's charity toward the poor:

> Many indigent persons who are unable to purchase wood
> or other necessaries of life, go to the poor-house, and
> ultimately prove an advantage to the establishment; these
> come and go when they choose: the homeless and all are
> taken in there. The paupers are mostly men and women

advanced in years, who work a little every day; they work at their ease, no one offering to extort more from them than they are able and willing to perform. It is surprising to witness how neat their farm and gardens appear. . . . This is the work of the men; the women stay within doors, they wash, iron, mend, and cook. . . . From 200 to 300 paupers are supported in this manner, annually, being little expense to the community. I never saw more happiness, ease and comfort, than exists in the poor-house in Boston.[5]

There were strong pacifist movements in New England too. Many people joined poets James Russell Lowell and Ralph Waldo Emerson in advocating universal peace and expressing opposition to the Mexican War of the 1840's. In 1847, responding to President James Polk's contention that Mexico had started the war, the Massachusetts legislature resolved that the war was one of conquest and unconstitutional in its origin and character. The legislature further resolved to oppose the war by "withholding supplies, or other voluntary contributions, for its further prosecution, by calling for the withdrawal of our army within the established limits of the United States, and in every just way aiding the country to retreat from the disgraceful position of aggression which it now occupies toward a weak, distracted neighbor and sister republic."

The ferment of change also affected religion. The Puritan tenets of duty to one's neighbor, personal responsibility to try to improve the environment, and insistence that one do his best at whatever his calling were given new applications. Emerson, who had been a minister until 1832, wrote that "reform is affirmative, conservatism negative; conservatism goes for comfort, reform for truth." And Henry David Thoreau, who turned from the manufacture of lead pencils to the study of nature and who personally seceded from the United States in protest against slavery, advised, "Do not be too moral. You may cheat yourself out of much life. Aim above morality. Be not simply good; be good for something."

Formerly, merchants had been the aristocrats of New

Essayist-poet Ralph Waldo Emerson was the literary spokesman for the nineteenth-century transcendental movement. He crusaded for individual freedom and self-reliance.

[5] Quoted in Tryon, *Native Land*, p. 61.

England. Now the factory system was producing a new leisure class. The influx of immigrants from Europe posed new problems and challenges to a changing New England society. Large-scale migrations to the West were spreading the ideas and attitudes of New England to other regions. And so were publishers. The novels and stories of James Fenimore Cooper, Herman Melville, Nathaniel Hawthorne, and Richard Henry Dana, the poetry of Emily Dickinson, John Greenleaf Whittier, William Cullen Bryant, Henry Wadsworth Longfellow, James Russell Lowell, and Oliver Wendell Holmes, Sr., and the essays of Emerson and Thoreau attest to the region's literary and intellectual vitality during the period from 1820 to 1860.

Daniel Webster, New England Statesman

New England's greatest statesman during the pre–Civil War period was Daniel Webster of Massachusetts. Beginning his political career as a Federalist, Webster reflected New England's opposition to the War of 1812, and many times later in his career he was forced to remember the veiled threats of disunion for which he had been responsible then. While New England remained a largely commercial region, Webster opposed congressional attempts to tax imported manufactures. But as a senator during the time when manufacturing began to be as important as commerce in his state, Webster favored protective tariffs.

Yet Webster also became a nationalist, a strong believer in the Union. This was dramatically demonstrated in 1830 when Senator Samuel A. Foot of Connecticut proposed a resolution to limit the sale of public lands in the West. Western senators denounced this proposal as part of a Yankee attempt to keep New England factory workers at home, drive wages down, and prevent the growth of the West. South Carolina's Senator Robert Hayne supported the western senators and proposed that the West and the South join forces to secure low prices for public lands as well as low tariffs to reduce the cost of manufactured goods. Webster defended the protective tariff while emphasizing New England's friendship for the West. Gradually, as the debate continued, the issue changed from tariffs and public

Transcendentalist Henry David Thoreau lived at Walden Pond, near Concord, Massachusetts, where he spent more than two years studying nature and recording his experiences in *Walden, or Life in the Woods.*

Daniel Webster of Massachusetts.

lands to states' rights and national powers. Hayne finally contended that there was no authority above that of the states. The Constitution, he said, was a compact between sovereign states from which they could withdraw whenever they chose. Webster denied this. The Constitution, he stated, was the supreme law of the land and the Supreme Court its final interpreter. "The inherent right in the people to reform their government I do not deny," Webster went on,

> and they have another right, and that is, to resist unconstitutional laws, without overturning the government. It is no doctrine of mine that unconstitutional laws bind the people. The great question is, whose prerogative is it to decide on

the constitutionality or unconstitutionality of the laws? On that, the main debate hinges. . . . The people of the United States have declared that this Constitution shall be the supreme law. We must either admit the proposition, or dispute their authority.

Webster performed his greatest act of statesmanship at the close of his political career in 1850. As a result of the acquisition of new lands following the war with Mexico, the issue of slavery in the territories came up again. Senator Henry Clay proposed a series of resolutions, known collectively as the Omnibus Bill or the Compromise of 1850, which were intended to permit California's entry into the Union as a free state and to provide a means of settling the question of slavery in other parts of the newly acquired territory.

Harriet Beecher Stowe's *Uncle Tom's Cabin* made people aware that slavery was not "a positive good," as John Calhoun had stated. The book did much to solidify northern sentiment against slavery, making the issue a moral one.

Under the provisions of the compromise, citizens of the new territories of Utah and New Mexico would decide the slavery question when they drew up state constitutions. Southern senators opposed this, although they favored another part of the compromise, the Fugitive Slave Bill. This legislation required the return of runaway slaves to their owners and provided fines, imprisonment, and the payment of damages to the owner upon conviction of anyone accused of aiding a fugitive slave.

Slave-catching and the possible spread of slavery were anathema to most northern senators. Any restrictions on the perpetuation and extension of slavery were abhorrent to southerners. The passionate debate over the Compromise of 1850 threatened to end the Union then and there, for southerners were talking openly of secession.

Daniel Webster had consistently supported the Wilmot Proviso of 1846, which sought to exclude slavery from any territory that might be acquired from Mexico. But when he arose in the Senate to speak in favor of the compromise on March 7, 1850, he demonstrated his conviction that the preservation of the Union was paramount over all other issues. And this conviction cost him the friendship of many New Englanders and all the abolitionists.

I wish to speak to-day, not as a Massachusetts man, nor

as a Northern man, but as an American. . . . I speak to-day for the preservation of the Union. . . . I hear with distress and anguish the word "secession," especially when it falls from the lips of those who are patriotic. . . . Secession! Peaceable secession! Sir, your eyes and mine are never destined to see that miracle. . . . Why, what would be the result? Where is the line to be drawn? What States are to secede? What is to remain American? What am I to be? An American no longer? Am I to become a sectional man, a local man, a separatist, with no country in common with the gentlemen who sit around me here, or fill the other house of Congress? Heaven forbid.

Webster's speech unquestionably affected public opinion in both the North and the South, and the compromise legislation was passed by Congress in September, 1850. Most historians agree that the Compromise of 1850 postponed the Civil War for ten years.

Cotton, Slaves, and China Trees

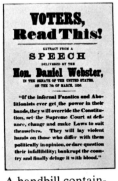

VOTERS, Read This!

EXTRACT FROM A

SPEECH

DELIVERED BY THE

Hon. Daniel Webster,

IN THE SENATE OF THE UNITED STATES, ON THE 7th OF MARCH, 1850.

"If the infernal Fanatics and Abolitionists ever get the power in their hands, they will override the Constitution, set the Supreme Court at defiance, change and make Laws to suit themselves. They will lay violent hands on those who differ with them politically in opinion, or dare question their infallibility; bankrupt the country and finally deluge it with blood."

A handbill containing an extract from Webster's Seventh of March speech.

The South was not a homogeneous unit geographically or socially. Its geography varied from the rounded, forested tops of the Appalachian chain to the muddy bayous along the Mississippi River and included the relatively flat and low coastal plain bounded by the piedmont on the one side and the Atlantic Ocean and the Gulf of Mexico on the other. The South had commercial and trading centers— New Orleans, Atlanta, Charleston, Memphis. It had a smattering of industry—turpentine and shoe factories, a few cotton mills—although in comparison with the North, industrialization in the South was practically nil. The people varied with the terrain and the economic activity. In the trading centers there were merchants as sharp and shrewd as any Yankee. A spirit of rugged individualism prevailed among the small farmers of the hill country where slavery, economically unfeasible, never took hold. Animosity and even antipathy between people of the back country and those of the coastal tidewater region had existed since colonial times. Economic and political differences between the two groups made eastern Tennessee more Union than

Courtesy of The Art Institute of Chicago

Slaves ginning and baling cotton on a southern plantation.

Confederate during the Civil War and caused the formation of West Virginia in 1861.

Political and economic control of the South, however,
rested in the leaders of tidewater society, as it had since
colonial days. Here, as it always had been, power was
rooted in one-crop agriculture. First it had been tobacco
in Virginia and indigo and rice in South Carolina. After
1820 it was cotton, and the Cotton Kingdom came to represent the South. Cotton dominated southern politics, economics, and society—the whole southern way of life.

The Cotton Belt began along the lower Potomac River
in Maryland and included the eastern half of Virginia,
northeastern North Carolina, nearly all of South Carolina,
central Georgia and Alabama, most of Mississippi, and the
Mississippi River regions of Louisiana, Arkansas, and Tennessee. The cotton-producing region has often been referred to as the Black Belt, a term especially appropriate
to the area west of the Appalachians, where the fertile

black soil and the large number of Negroes in the population combined to give double meaning to the term.

In any listing of the events responsible for setting North and South on a collision course, it would be necessary to include the invention of the cotton gin in 1793. Until then, cotton production had been an unprofitable enterprise. The hours of tedious hand labor required to separate fiber from seed had discouraged southern farmers and planters from growing the crop. Within sixty years after the appearance of Eli Whitney's invention, cotton completely dominated the southern economy. By the 1850's, it had brought considerable prosperity to the region, along with an arrogant belief in cotton's importance and influence. In 1855 Senator James H. Hammond of South Carolina posed the question: "What would happen if no cotton was furnished for three years?" His answer introduced an idea that would help lead the South out of the Union, "I will not stop to depict what everyone can imagine," Hammond went on, "but this is certain: England would topple headlong and carry the whole civilized world with her. No, you dare not make war on cotton. No power on earth dares to make war upon it. Cotton is King!"

As New England's influence extended to the West, the cotton culture of the southern Atlantic states spread beyond the Appalachian barrier into the Gulf Basin and across the Mississippi River to Texas. The older southern states experienced population losses even more severe than those of New England during the decades before the Civil War. By 1850, the populations of Alabama, Mississippi, Louisiana, and Arkansas nearly equaled those of the older states. The older states, whose land had been worn out by years of tobacco cultivation, could not compete against the lure of cheaper and more fertile lands to the west. And the people who moved took the institution of slavery with them.

Southern cities were small and slow-paced compared to those in the North. Mrs. Anne Royall's description of Savannah, Georgia, contrasted sharply with her accounts of New England cities, which, as she noted, were bustling commercial centers.

The streets of Savannah are one sea of sand; the novelty

of this, and the pride of China [trees] in full bloom, filling
the air with the sweetest fragrance, the profusion of its
foliage, and the soft tinge of its exuberant flowers, the hum
of insects, the fruit shops, the genial shade, and the pleasant
sunshine—I have no name for the scene!

Savannah is the garden spot of the South, whether as
to opulence, trade, refinement, hospitality, or site. The
buildings of Savannah are rather indifferent, like those of
Charleston [South Carolina] and much inferior to those of
Augusta [Georgia]. They seem to take most pride in deco-
rating their streets with those beautiful trees. . . .[6]

The business of Savannah, as of most Southern cities,
was directly associated with buying, selling, and transport-
ing cotton, rice, or tobacco.

The business season commences late in the fall, and ends
in June, and such is their industry, that they scarcely leave
time for refreshment or repose. After the business season
is over, they then enjoy themselves with their friends—
travel to the north, or amuse themselves as they please, till
the business season comes round again. This is the routine
of all the southern towns. . . .

From the top of the Exchange, we have one of the handsomest prospects in the southern country, and by a long
way the most extensive. For the distance of eight miles,
you see one continued plain of rice and cotton fields.
Splendid mansions, groves of live oak, magnolia gardens,
the river with its islands, steamboats, and shipping,
the whole city with its squares and regular streets,
lined with [China trees], with the endless cotton ware-
houses . . . present to the eye, a most ravishing picture
of beauty, or rather novelty to a traveller.

The Exchange Mrs. Royall referred to was a building
that contained many of Savannah's business and commercial offices. In discussing southern towns in general, Joseph
H. Ingraham, a New England novelist who married the
daughter of a wealthy Mississippi planter and toured the
South in 1835, described them as more

[6] Quoted in ibid., p. 60.
[7] Quoted in ibid., p. 153.

Library of Congress

Slaves preparing cotton for ginning on the Smith plantation near Beaufort, South Carolina, in 1862.

properly the "Exchange" for the neighbouring planters, and the "Broadway" for their wives and daughters. . . . Each town is the centre of a circle which extends many miles around it into the country, and daily attracts all within its influence. The ladies come in their carriages "to shop," the gentlemen, on horseback, to do business with their commission merchants, visit the banks, hear the news, dine together at the hotels, and ride back in the evening.[s]

The South was cotton and slaves. The region's wealth was invested in land and chattels, not in banking, industry, or transportation. Cotton was vital to the South's economy, and its production, so southerners believed, required a

[s] Quoted in ibid., pp. 153–154.

plantation system in which the work of cultivating and harvesting the fiber was done by slave labor. As a result, nearly all segments of southern society eventually defended slavery.

The white population of the South contained a larger percentage of Anglo-Saxons than the population of the North. There were comparatively few foreign-born citizens in the South, owing mainly to the lack of industry and jobs and the existence of slave-labor competition. The South was not attractive to most European immigrants.

Historian Allan Nevins has written that to a far greater degree than the North, the South was a land of class stratification which retained vestiges of feudalism; life in the South was more aristocratic in its tone than life in the North. Professor Nevins identifies the lack of a large group of intelligent, independent, thoughtful, and educated farmers to match a similar body in the North as the central weakness of the South.

At the top of Southern class structure were about 8,000 planters who owned more than fifty slaves each, and certain professional persons—mostly lawyers and merchants—who depended on the cotton industry. Just below this class was a large group of white families owning from one to fifty slaves. Many more white families owned no slaves at all. The so-called "mountain whites" who farmed the valleys, or coves, of the southern Appalachians were examples of nonslaveholding whites. There were also small farms here and there on the lowlands owned by whites who for the most part were poor, illiterate, and nonslaveholders. These people lived in what could be called rural slums.

How can one account for the development of the southern class structure? Some historians cite the moderate climate and the fertile soil of the South. The region was well suited to large-scale, single-crop agriculture, a system which has usually produced large, almost baronial estates in which strong aristocratic traditions, manners, and behavior develop. Southerners were able to transplant and maintain notions of class that existed in the nonindustrial parts of England where the country squire stood at the top of the social pyramid, and where there were few opportunities for the low-born to rise in wealth and status. Frederick Law Olmsted wrote of a plantation he visited in eastern Virginia in the 1850's:

> The labor of this farm was entirely performed by slaves. I did not inquire their number, but I judged there were from twenty to forty. . . .
>
> During three hours, or more, in which I was in company with the proprietor, I do not think there were ten consecutive minutes uninterrupted by some of the slaves requiring his personal direction or assistance. He was even obliged, three times, to leave the dinner-table.
>
> "You see," said he, smiling, as he came in the last time, "a farmer's life, in this country, is no sinecure." Thus turning the conversation to Slavery, he observed, in answer to a remark of mine, "I only wish your philanthropists would contrive some satisfactory plan to relieve us of it; the trouble and the responsibility of properly taking care of our negroes, you may judge, from what you see yourself here, is anything but enviable. But what can we do that is better? Our free negroes—and, I believe it is the same at the North as it is here—are a miserable set of vagabonds, drunken, vicious, worse off, it is my honest opinion, than those who are retained in slavery. I am satisfied, too, that our slaves are better off, as they are, than the majority of your free laboring classes at the North.[9]

Many planters, particularly those in the older regions of the Cotton Kingdom, expressed similar desires to rid themselves of the responsibilities related to the use of slave labor. But few believed that a plantation could be operated profitably with hired labor.

Owners of large plantations commonly employed overseers to supervise the field work of the slaves. Said Olmsted:

> Each overseer regulated the hours of work on his own plantation. I saw the negroes at work before sunrise and after sunset. At about eight o'clock they were allowed to stop for breakfast, and again about noon, to dine. The

---

[9] Quoted in ibid., p. 184.

A gang of slaves, journeying to be sold in a southern market.

length of these rests was at the discretion of the overseer or drivers. . . . The number of hands directed by each overseer was considerably over one hundred. The manager [planter] thought it would be better economy to have a white man over every fifty hands, but the difficulty of obtaining trustworthy overseers prevented it. Three of those he then had were the best he had ever known. He described the great majority as being passionate, careless, inefficient men, generally intemperate, and totally unfitted for the duties of the position. The best overseers, ordinarily, are young men, the sons of small planters, who take up the business temporarily, as a means of acquiring a little capital with which to purchase negroes for themselves.[10]

Despite the responsibilities and problems of the position, the apparent ambition of most young men of the South

[10] Quoted in ibid., pp. 207–208.

was to become a wealthy planter. Many successful doctors, lawyers, and even ministers left their professions once they were financially able to establish themselves as planters. Northern visitors were often surprised to find many of the professional men of the South relatively young and inexperienced. Few men without professional training, capital, or family ties were able to achieve the aristocratic status of the leading planter families.

Marriages between members of wealthy families helped to perpetuate the aristocracy. As a result, pride in family lineage, traditions of chivalry, and sensitivity to family honor were as important among the planter aristocracy of the South as they were among great landholding families of England.

The responsibilities of the mistress of the plantation were also demanding. Henry C. Knight, a young New Englander who spent five years touring the South, gave the following account:

> . . . The mistress usually carries about a ponderous bunch of keys; as articles are kept under lock from the slaves, and doled out each day for use. Where there are children, each single babe, if there be a dozen, has its particular nurse, or black mamma; to spy it, and tote it up and down all day upon her shoulder, until it is three or four years old. The matrons, in the upper classes, are industrious, affable, and accomplished, in a high degree. The young ladies, with their pensive, but imaginative countenances, frequently dip into the heart. What is amiable, I have seen a little miss sit down at the side-table, on an evening, to instruct an aged houseslave to spell in the Bible.[11]

Taken as a whole, and including Negroes who comprised the majority of the population in some areas, the illiteracy rate of the South was five times that of New England. In many areas, planter families provided the only example of culture and education. Many planters' sons and daughters finished their education in the numerous private high schools of the South, for there were no public schools until

[11] Quoted in ibid., p. 227.

after the Civil War. If there was no private academy nearby, a planter often hired a family tutor—usually a New Englander. Eli Whitney, for example, was on his way to a teaching job in the South when he grew interested in the problem of ginning cotton.

The South had several institutions of higher education, among them the College of William and Mary, the University of Virginia, and the Virginia Military Institute, often called "the West Point of the South." A number of planters, on the other hand, established and maintained a family tradition of sending their sons to England for a college education.

There was little or no schooling for members of other classes. As Professor Nevins has said, "The South was for the most part a land where the poor man's son was likely to go untaught, and the workingman or small farmer to be ignorant if not illiterate."[12]

Local and state governments in the South were dominated by the slaveholding planters. Because southern legislatures, in many instances, elected the governor, state officers, and important members of the state judicial systems, the planters maintained control of all branches of government. They firmly believed that men who owned property—land and slaves—had a greater stake in society than the landless and were therefore entitled to governmental power and to the advantages that power gave them.

Many planters were men of education and culture, but their main interest and contributions were in politics, not in the fields of literature, the arts, or science. The isolation of life on the plantations and the absence of large cities with their intellectual stimulation help explain why the Cotton Kingdom failed to produce an Emerson or a Thoreau. The planters' preference in literature ran more to the romantic tales of knighthood and chivalry found in the poems and novels of Sir Walter Scott and Lord Byron.

Individualistic, romantic, snobbish, and *unrealistic* were a few of the characteristics attributed to the southern

[12] Quoted in Kenneth Stampp, ed., *The Causes of the Civil War* (Englewood Cliffs, N.J.: Prentice-Hall, 1959), p. 171.

For plantation owners and their families, life along the Mississippi was comfortable and very social—a continuous round of visits, parties, and dances.

planter. In his critical analysis, *The Mind of the South,* W. J. Cash poses the question: "Why had the South, which by the 1850's enjoyed riches, rank, and a leisure perhaps unmatched elsewhere in the world, not progressed to a complex and important intellectual culture . . . ?" Cash answers in this way:

> . . . The Southern world . . . was basically an extremely uncomplex, unvaried, and unchanging one. Here economic and political organization was reduced to its simplest elements. Here were no towns to rank as more than trading posts [or] mere depots on the road to the markets of the world, mere adjuncts to the plantation. . . . Here was lacking even that tremendous ferment of immigration which was so important in lending variety to the rest of the American scene . . . a world in which horses, dogs, guns, not books, and ideas and art, were [the planter's] normal and absorbing interests.[13]

Below the numerically small but extremely influential planter class were the groups of plain farmers with few if any slaves and the mountain and poor whites who owned no slaves at all. These people were not generally hard-

[13] W. J. Cash, *The Mind of the South* (New York: Alfred A. Knopf, 1941), pp. 98, 99.

driving and ambitious; a Yankee farmer would have called them shiftless and lazy. Growing cotton, tobacco, and corn required but three or four months' work at the most, and a man who owned some land could insure with a minimum of effort that he and his family would never actually go hungry.

Most mountain whites were descendants of English or Scots-Irish families who had crossed the southern Appalachians and settled in isolated valleys. Cut off from the Cotton Kingdom, these people were largely ignorant of the world outside their coves. Because of inbreeding and geographic isolation, they represented what historian Frederick Jackson Turner called a "retarded frontier." Their lives revolved around clan feuds, moonshine whisky, religious revival and camp meetings, husking and quilting bees, and house raisings. They wore homespun clothing and lived in log cabins. These people were intensely democratic and egalitarian. They hated slavery and the slaveholders who controlled the state governments.

Frederick Law Olmsted visited the mountain whites and wrote of their way of life:

> The women, as well as the men, generally smoke, and tobacco is grown for home use. They are more industrious than the men, often being seen at work in the fields, and at spinning wheels and hand-looms in almost every house. I was less troubled by vermin than in the low country, yet so much so that I adopted the habit of passing the night on the floor of the cabins, rather than in their beds. The furniture of the cabins is rather less meager than that of a similar class of habitations in the lower region . . . it is common to see a square frame in which are piled a dozen bed quilts. Notwithstanding the ignorance of the people, books are more common than even in the houses of the slave owners of the planting districts.[14]

If there was a middle class in the South, it was made up of the large number of independent farmers who worked their own lands or, if they owned a slave or two, labored

[14] Quoted in Tryon, *Native Land*, p. 222.

alongside them in the fields. Persuaded that their own well-being depended on the prosperity of their planter neighbors, however, they could usually be counted on to support the political and economic beliefs of the aristocracy. W. J. Cash has noted how independent farmers were influenced by aristocratic ideals:

> Indeed, I am not sure that the most fortunate result of all
> in this field is not to be found in the case of the better sort
> of those yeoman farmers who stood between the planters
> and the true poor whites; . . . there was no claim to personal
> aristocracy. But therein lay its strength. These men took
> from aristocracy as much as, and no more than, could be
> made to fit with their own homespun qualities; and so what
> they took they made solidly their own, without any sense
> of inadequacy to haunt them into [social awkwardness]. The
> result was a kindly courtesy, a level-eyed pride, an easy
> quietness, a barely perceptible flourish of bearing, which,
> for all its obvious angularity and fundamental plainness,
> was one of the finest things the Old South produced.[15]

At the bottom of the social scale were the poor whites who lived outside the mountains. Negroes scorned them as "poor white trash," and white planters and farmers referred to them as "crackers" and "clay-eaters." These people lived on the most inferior or worn-out lands of the South. They suffered from malaria, hookworm, and malnutrition much of the time. They looked upon manual labor as an obnoxious activity and supported slavery because of a belief in racial superiority.

Joseph H. Ingraham met a number of teamsters while visiting Mississippi River towns in 1835. The men were poor whites who had driven wagonloads of cotton from eastern Mississippi to the market at Vicksburg. Ingraham wrote of these people:

> With the awkwardness of the Yankee countryman, they are
> destitute of his morals, education, and reverence for re-
> ligion. With the rude and bold qualities of the chivalrous

---

[15] Cash, *Mind of the South*, p. 72.

Kentuckian, they are destitute of his intelligence, and the humour which tempers and renders amusing his very vices. They are in general uneducated, and their apparel consists of a coarse linsey-woolsey, of a dingy yellow or blue, with broad-brimmed hats, though they usually follow their teams barefooted and bare-headed, with their long locks hanging over their eyes and shoulders, giving them a wild appearance. . . . They are good hunters, and expert with the rifle, which is an important article of furniture in their houses. Whiskey is their favourite beverage, which they present to the stranger with one hand, while they give him a chair with the other.[16]

The South after 1830, continuing to depend on a one-crop agricultural economy, became even more stratified in its social structure. Its leisure class was the product of a slave-labor system and its middle class was largely illiterate. The section was dominated by a planter aristocracy which opposed change and firmly believed that the North wished to deprive the South of equality in the Union.

Because the section was in these many ways unique does not mean that southerners did not love the Union. Many men of the South had given their lives in the Revolution, in the War of 1812, and in the Mexican War. But southerners did not seem to think of the Union in the same terms northerners did. They felt that their institutions, customs, and way of life were threatened by the trend toward a more unified and, to them, an increasingly alien nation.

John C. Calhoun, Southern Statesman

John C. Calhoun of South Carolina was the spokesman of the South between 1830 and 1850. Like Daniel Webster, Calhoun served in both houses of Congress and aspired to the presidency. Both men were recognized for their intellect and their eloquence as speakers. As acknowledged spokesmen of their sections, over the years both reversed their positions on the fundamental political question of nationalism versus states' rights. Despite these parallels, the

[16] Quoted in Tryon, *Native Land*, pp. 204–205.

John C. Calhoun.

political careers of these two men provide direct contrasts.

As a fervent nationalist, the young Calhoun had advocated war in 1812, voted for military establishments, and supported a high tariff on the grounds that it would help tie the republic more closely together. Calhoun then favored the "American System" of internal improvements at federal expense that would provide a network of canals and railroads throughout the nation.

President James Madison appointed Calhoun secretary of war in 1817, and, until he was elected vice-president under John Quincy Adams seven years later, Calhoun lived in Washington. But in 1825, when he returned to South Carolina and bought a plantation, Calhoun's political philosophy began to change. The man who had been an outspoken nationalist became the most vocal defender of the doctrine of state supremacy over the authority of the federal government. His new political theory included the fundamental premise of human inequality.

The reason for the change in Calhoun's political philosophy can be found in South Carolina's changing prospects in the Union. The traditional supremacy of South Carolina and the South generally in the federal government was being seriously challenged by the rapidly industrializing North. The South, destined to remain agrarian, might not be able to prevent the passage of economic legislation favorable to northern interests but detrimental to its own. The tariff controversy exemplified this conflict. Northern industrialists wanted tariffs on imported goods in order to reduce competition from foreign manufacturers. But to South Carolinians, with little industry of their own, tariffs would bring no economic advantage—on the contrary, tariffs meant higher prices on the manufactured goods they had to buy. In 1828, Calhoun anonymously published his *South Carolina Exposition* in protest against the high tariff passed that year. He was still vice-president when he introduced, through this essay, the ideas of nullification and interposition.

Calhoun maintained that the Union was a voluntary partnership composed of states that retained the right to decide the constitutionality of federal laws. According to him, a state legislature could nullify a federal law its members considered unconstitutional and could forbid its enforcement within the state. Calhoun's principle of interposition held that if any state nullified a federal law, three-fourths of all the states must approve that law by constitutional amendment before it could be enforced. The states could interpose themselves between the federal government and the people.

Calhoun had not put his name on *The South Carolina Exposition*. In the address he gave on nullification and interposition in 1831, he took his first public stand on the issue of states' rights:

> This right of interposition . . . be it called what it may,— State-right, veto, nullification, or by any other name,—I conceive to be the fundamental principle of our system, resting on facts historically as certain as our revolution itself, and deductions as simple and demonstrative as that of any political or moral truth whatever; and I firmly believe that on its recognition depend the stability and safety of our political institutions.

In 1832 the South Carolina legislature declared the tariff of 1828 unconstitutional and adopted an ordinance of nullification. Calhoun's state also threatened to secede from the Union if attempts were made to enforce the tariff in South Carolina. President Andrew Jackson reacted quickly and decisively. In his "Proclamation to the People of South Carolina" he said:

> I consider . . . the power to annul a law of the United States, assumed by one State, incompatible with the existence of the Union, contradicted expressly by the letter of the Constitution, unauthorized by its spirit, inconsistent with every principle on which it was founded, and destructive of the great object for which it was formed.

Jackson had privately informed some of Calhoun's South Carolina friends that "if one drop of blood be shed there in defiance of the laws of the United States, I will hang the first man of them I can get my hands on to the first tree I can find."

The issue was settled by compromise. Henry Clay and Calhoun together worked out a new tariff that would gradually reduce rates over a ten-year period. Congress then passed both the tariff bill and the Force Bill, which granted the president authority over the South Carolina militia as well as over federal troops. A second convention met in South Carolina, revoked the nullification ordinance, and then nullified the Force Act. There the matter rested.

Calhoun resigned the vice-presidency and was elected to the Senate. There he continued to wage his battle against what he considered the majority's oppression of the minority, the grinding away of states' rights and power by the federal government. And there he developed his much-publicized view that slavery, far from being an evil institution, was a positive good.

In 1848 Calhoun opposed the Wilmot Proviso that would have prohibited slavery in the territory acquired from Mexico. He defended the southern demand that Congress permit and protect slavery in all the territories. Calhoun realized that slavery itself could not succeed in the western lands, for the possibility of developing a plantation agriculture there was slight; his real concern was to preserve the balance of slave states and free states in the Senate.

The last public meeting of the great triumvirate—Clay, Webster, and Calhoun—occurred during the sectional crisis of 1850, when Henry Clay's compromise was argued. Calhoun—ill, feeble, and only weeks away from death—had a fellow senator read his speech for him. He warned that the Union was endangered by antislavery agitation and by northern discrimination against the South. What would preserve the Union? Calhoun listed the necessary actions: (1) guarantee the South security within the Union; (2) return runaway slaves; (3) stop antislavery agitation; and (4) amend the Constitution to provide protection for the South. Calhoun proposed the establishment of a dual presidency, one president to be elected by the North and the other by the South, each having veto power over all federal legislation.

What did Calhoun do for the South? This is Richard N. Current's evaluation of his career:

Henry Clay proposing the Compromise of 1850 to the Senate. Calhoun is standing, third from right, facing Clay; Webster is seated behind Clay, head in hand.

"The South! The poor South!" Calhoun had exclaimed upon his deathbed. Certainly he had meant well for his section, his homeland. Yet by his very efforts to preserve the way of life he loved, he had helped to prepare the way for its ultimate destruction. No man had done more than he to arouse the North, divide the national political parties . . . justify state sovereignty . . . and persuade Southerners that extreme measures were peaceful and constitutional when, as events were to demonstrate, such measures could lead only to war. In the desolated South of 1865 it could aptly have been said of Calhoun: if you seek his monument, look about you.[17]

Saul K. Padover suggests a lesson to be learned from a study of Calhoun's life:

On April 12, 1861, eleven years after Calhoun's death,

[17] Richard N. Current, *John C. Calhoun* (New York: Washington Square Press, 1963), p. 34.

his native state, speaking through the cannon of Fort Sumter, gave irrevocable voice to his ultimate commitments. Calhoun's cause died in a welter of fratricidal blood, but his personality lives as a monumental reminder that the ideal of equality and democracy needs constant defense against grim and sincere critics—such as the formidable senator from South Carolina.[18]

Land of Mountains, Plains, and Deserts

The decades of the 1830's and 1840's witnessed the most rapid expansion of the frontier in the nation's history. Not since the Louisiana Purchase, which took in an area the frontier had just begun to reach, had such vast amounts of land been added to the national domain. Texas was annexed in 1845; a treaty with Britain gave the United States clear title to the Pacific Northwest in 1846; and New Mexico, California, and the deserts of the Great Basin were ceded to the United States by Mexico in 1848.

In 1830, the frontier lay along the Mississippi River. The Old Northwest Territory had by this time produced the states of Ohio, Indiana, and Illinois. Michigan was to achieve statehood within the decade. During the 1830's and 1840's, steamboats converted the great rivers of the West—the Ohio, Tennessee, Cumberland, Wabash, and the Mississippi—into highways. One eastern visitor wrote:

> To me who has never visited the public wharves of the great cities of the West, it is no trivial task to convey an adequate idea of the spectacle they present. The commerce of the Eastern seaports and that of the Western Valleys are utterly dissimilar; not more in the staples of intercourse than in the mode in which it is conducted; and, were one desirous of exhibiting to a friend from the Atlantic shore a picture of the prominent features which characterize commercial proceedings upon the Western waters, or, indeed, of Western character in its general outline, he could do no

[18] Saul K. Padover, *The Genius of America* (New York: McGraw-Hill, 1960), p. 155. Copyright © 1960 by Saul K. Padover. Used with permission of McGraw-Hill Book Company.

Tulane University

A sidewheel steamboat unloading its cargo at the Sugar Levee, New Orleans, 1853.

better than to place him in the wild uproar of the steamboat quay.[19]

While Memphis, New Orleans, and other cities of the
lower Mississippi were becoming important commercial and
cosmopolitan centers, men were building railroads north of
the Ohio River. In 1854 the railroads reached the Mississippi and within two years they were across it and pushing rapidly west toward the Missouri. This great east-west
network of railroads ended the West's dependence on the
Mississippi River as its primary artery of travel and commerce. Economically the West was now tied securely to the
North, not the South.

What about the Far West between 1830 and 1850?
During these two decades the frontier reached the Missouri

[19] Quoted in Tryon, *Native Land*, p. 305.

The Metropolitan Museum of Art

In 1853, Independence, Missouri, was one of the last "civilized" stops on the long trail west to California and Oregon.

River where it ceased to be one identifiable line. It fragmented instead into numerous frontiers, each with a slightly different purpose for its existence, each with a different character, but with the people of all predominantly Union in sentiment. A few of those frontiers will be briefly examined here.

Missouri to Santa Fe

Beyond the Mississippi, the nation's westward expansion at first followed the Missouri River. It was along this river that Oregon-bound travelers and Santa Fe-bound traders made up their caravans of wagons. A visitor to Missouri's capital in 1848 described activities at the Jefferson City court house:

The session of Court attracted a considerable number of country people to the town. . . . A rougher set of citizens, whether regarded with reference to dress, manners or physical appearance, separately or combined, could not be imagined. Bearskin caps, Mackinaw blankets, leather leggings, old Bess rifles and hunting knives, entered into their dress and equipments. Tall, square-shouldered, broad-chested, stout men, made up of bone and gristle, they drank whiskey, chewed tobacco, and while waiting for the opening of Court, engaged in athletic sports. . . . The Court was not unfrequently adjourned for a buffalo hunt, and the business of the day was always dispatched, that the judge and the bar might spend a part of the afternoon pitching quoits. Their evenings were passed over the whist-table, or in political discussions; they often indulged in roseate views of the future of the United States, and prognosticated . . . on what the Editor of the Jefferson paper, Mr. Windett (a Yankee importation), called "our Almighty country."[20]

At the other end of the Santa Fe Trail, along the upper Rio Grande, 780 miles away, inhabitants of Mexican settlements were eager to exchange silver dollars for Yankee goods. This trade continued and came firmly under American control during the Mexican War. Although a brief but bloody revolt against United States authority occurred the next year at Taos, General Stephen W. Kearny's Army of the West marched into Santa Fe's plaza unopposed on August 18, 1846. Two years later, the Treaty of Guadalupe Hidalgo officially placed the Pueblo Indians and the Spanish people of the Santa Fe area under United States control. At that time, as Paul Horgan has written:

Santa Fe was shabby, with no signs of either taste or wealth. There were no gardens—but the visitors had not yet looked within patio walls. Cornfields were laid out in the very center of town. Everything was a queer jumble of the clever and the primitive. Public walks enclosing the plaza were covered by a continuous roof, which was capital in case of rain; but there were no "public lights" anywhere in the streets at night. Delicious fruits were to be had at the market—peaches, grapes, melons, apples. The residents were poor and beggarly, and if the women were not hand-

[20] Quoted in ibid., p. 322.

some, they were "rather more intelligent than the men" and all loved parties, for there were "phandagoes almost every night." . . . If there was one general impression shared by all, it was about the bells. There were five in the main church, and the other two had one or more each, and they all rang, it seemed, all the time, night and day. Dawdling about the famous old city, a soldier decided that in what he saw there was "nothing to pay us for our long march. . . ."[21]

The Trek to the Great Salt Lake

The Mormons' leader, Brigham Young.

Persecution of the Mormons in Missouri and then in Illinois convinced Brigham Young, who had taken over leadership from the murdered Joseph Smith, that he must lead his people to a region where they could build their society unmolested. With the help of the Indian trader and mountain man, Jim Bridger, Young selected the Salt Lake Valley as the site of the New Zion. He led the first contingent of Latter Day Saints families across the plains and through a pass in the Wasatch Mountains into this desert region in the summer of 1847.

At first glance, the valley held little promise for a group of people who wished to base their way of life on agriculture. But because they were a closely knit group held together by religious zeal, willing to work cooperatively and make sacrifices, they succeeded in establishing themselves in the Far West. A decade after the industrious and frugal Mormons first turned mountain streams into their irrigation ditches, planted their first crops and fruit trees, and built their first adobe-brick houses, the editor of the *New York Tribune,* Horace Greeley, paid a visit to Salt Lake City. Life there was still hard and somewhat tenuous, yet to Greeley it appeared that the Mormons would persist and succeed.

Doubtless this city is far ahead of any rival, being the spiritual metropolis and the earliest settled. Its broad, regular streets, refreshed by rivulets of bright, sparkling, dancing

[21] Paul Horgan, *Great River: The Rio Grande in North American History*, 2 vols. (New York: Holt, Rinehart & Winston, 1954), 2: 730.

The Mormon settlement at Salt Lake City, 1853.

water, and shaded by rows of young but thrifty trees . . . are already more more attractive to the eye than those of an average city of like size in the states. . . . Undoubtedly, this people are steadily increasing in wealth and comfort.

Still the average life in Utah is a hard one. Many more days' faithful labor are required to support a family here than in Kansas, or in any of the states. The climate is severe and capricious—now intensely hot and dry; in winter cold and stormy; and, though cattle are usually allowed to shift for themselves in the valleys, they are apt to resent the insult by dying. Crickets and grasshoppers swarm in myriads, and often devour all before them. Wood is scarce and poor. Irrigation is laborious and expensive. . . . Frost is very destructive here; Indian corn rarely escapes it wholly, and wheat often suffers from it. . . . I estimate that one hundred fifty days' faithful labor in Kansas will produce as large an aggregate of the necessaries of life—food, clothing, fuel—as three hundred just such days' work in Utah. Hence, the adults here generally wear a toil-worn, anxious look, and many of them are older in frame than in years.[22]

California and Gold

New England ships' captains and sailors had been fa-

[22] Quoted in Tryon, *Native Land*, pp. 401–402.

miliar with California's coastal settlements long before gold was discovered. They had, for years past, anchored their ships along the coast side and traded Yankee goods to Spaniards and Indians in the mission stations and small towns in return for hides, tallow, and beaver pelts. The few American mountain men who had entered California's valleys in search of beaver had been welcomed by mission priests and they had been impressed with the pleasant lives wealthy ranchers led. Americans had also been impressed with the region's bountiful resources and moderate climate, the easy-going natives, and the Mexican government's neglect of California.

At the time James Marshall discovered shiny objects in the bottom of John Sutter's millrace, in 1848, the site of San Francisco held little of importance. It was occupied by a mission, a presidio—a garrison—and the tiny town of Paraje de Yerba Buena—place of good grass—which contained but twelve houses and only fifty inhabitants. Thanks to the discovery of gold, within a year the area had changed drastically:

By nine o'clock the town is in the full flow of business. The streets running down to the water, and Montgomery Street which fronts the Bay, are crowded with people, all in hurried motion. The variety of characters and costumes is remarkable. Our own countrymen seem to lose their local peculiarities in such a crowd, and it is by chance epithets rather than by manner, that the New-Yorker is distinguished from the Kentuckian, the Carolinian from the Down-Easter, the Virginian from the Texan. The German and Frenchmen are more easily recognized. Peruvians and Chilians go by in their brown ponchos, and the sober Chinese, cool and impassive in the midst of excitement, look out of the oblique corners of their long eyes at the bustle, but are never tempted to venture from their own line of business. The eastern side of the plaza, in front of the Parker House and a canvas hall called the Eldorado, are the general rendezvous of business and amusement—combining [ex]change, park, club-room and promenade all in one. . . . The character of the groups scattered along the plaza is oftentimes very in-

The New York Historical Society

The San Francisco waterfront, about 1851.

teresting. In one place are three or four speculators bargaining for lots, buying and selling "fifty varas square" in towns, some of which are canvas and some only paper; in another, a company of miners, brown as leather, and rugged in features as in dress; in a third, perhaps, three or four naval officers speculating on the next cruise, or a knot of genteel gamblers, talking over the last night's operations.[23]

The Far West of the 1850's was mostly a raw, untamed region, where law and order depended mainly on an individual's ability to take care of himself. The area around San Francisco was not the only one affected by gold fever. The discovery of yellow dust and nuggets near Denver, Colorado, in 1856 lured many prospectors to that area and stimulated the development of boom towns. Two decades later, the process would be repeated in the Black Hills of South Dakota. In 1850 California became the first state to be formed from territory in the Far West, and Oregon followed in 1859.

To a great extent, sectional rivalry involved attempts by the North and the South to dominate, or control, the West. Leaders of both sections wanted western votes in Congress

[23] Quoted in ibid., p. 382.

to help them further their own constituents' political, economic, and social aims. Until 1850, the South seemed to be more than holding its own in this struggle. Since the formation of the Union, the South had gained nine states to the North's eight. Slave states admitted after 1787 included Kentucky, Tennessee, Louisiana, Florida, Missouri, Alabama, Mississippi, Arkansas, and Texas. The new free states were Maine, Ohio, Indiana, Illinois, Michigan, Iowa, Wisconsin, and California. In terms of area, southern territorial expansion had far exceeded that of the North: 677,000 square miles of new slave territory to 346,856 square miles of free territory. The North, however, had the greater population: 22 million in 1860 to 9.5 million in the South, slaves representing one-third of that number.

Northern leaders considered the annexation of Texas in 1845 a southern attempt to expand the Cotton Kingdom and the influence of the South in political and economic affairs. New Englanders vigorously opposed the resulting war with Mexico. As has been pointed out, in 1847 the Massachusetts legislature passed a series of resolutions against that war, proclaiming that its purpose was to "strengthen the Slave Power and to open new markets for slavery."

Despite this opposition from New England—and also from such Whigs in Congress as Abraham Lincoln—the war with Mexico was fought to a successful conclusion and a large area was added to the United States. The question then became: which section will benefit from this huge acquisition? A glance at the geography of the Southwest, which included all the territory west of central Texas, revealed that the climate and aridity made the further expansion of the Cotton Kingdom improbable. The great compromiser, Henry Clay, took this into consideration when he drew up the provisions of his Compromise of 1850. Daniel Webster realized this when he agreed to support Clay's compromise at the risk of his political career. John C. Calhoun undoubtedly considered this when he rejected the compromise and demanded, instead, a dual presidency.

If these three leaders were aware that the Cotton Kingdom had, in fact, reached its limit of expansion, could they have taken any other positions than the ones they did on this great sectional issue? This is a question all students of the Civil War must grapple with.

SUGGESTED READINGS

Cash, W. J. *The Mind of the South.* Random House, Vintage Books.

Current, Richard N. *Daniel Webster and the Rise of National Conservatism.* Little, Brown.

De Tocqueville, Alexis. *Democracy in America.* Edited by J. P. Mayer. Doubleday, Anchor Books.

De Voto, Bernard. *Across the Wide Missouri.* Houghton Mifflin, Sentry Editions.

Eaton, Clement. *Henry Clay and the Art of American Politics.* Little, Brown.

Eaton, Clement. *The Growth of Southern Civilization, 1790–1860.* Harper & Row, Torchbooks.

Eaton, Clement. *The Mind of the Old South.* Louisiana State University Press.

Fehrenbacher, Don. *Manifest Destiny and the Coming of the Civil War, 1841–1860.* Appleton-Century-Crofts.

Horgan, Paul. *Great River: The Rio Grande in North American History.* 2 vols. Funk & Wagnalls, Minerva Press.

Olmsted, Frederick Law. *The Slave States Before the Civil War.* G. P. Putnam's Sons, Capricorn Books.

Rothe, Bertha, ed. *The Daniel Webster Reader.* Oceana, Docket Series.

Taylor, William R. *Cavalier and Yankee.* Harper & Row.

Thoreau, Henry David. *Thoreau: People, Principles and Politics.* Edited by M. Meltzer. Hill & Wang, American Century Series.

Tryon, W. S., ed. *My Native Land: Life in America, 1790–1870.* University of Chicago Press, Phoenix Books.

Woodham-Smith, Cecil. *The Great Hunger.* New American Library, Signet Books.

Woodward, C. Vann. *The Burden of Southern History.* New American Library, Mentor Books.

An invoice of ten negroes sent this day to John
B Williamson by Geo Kremer named & cost as fol—
lows

To wit Betsey Hackley $410.00
    Nancy Aulick 515.00
    Harry & Helen Miller . . 1200.00
    Mary Kootz 600.00
    Betsey Ott? 560.00
    Isaac & Fanny Brent . . 992.00
    Lucinda Luckett 467.50
    George Smith 510.00
Amount of my traveling expences & boarding 5254.50
of lot No 9 not included in the other bills . 39.50
    Kremers expences Transporting lot No to Chicks? 51.00
        Carryall hire 6.00
                            $5351.00

I have this day delivered the above named negroes
costing including my expences and other expences
five thousand three hundred & fifty dollars this May
26th 1835
                            John W. Pitman

I did intend to leave Nancy child but she made
such a damned fuss I had to let her take it I could
of got fifty Dollars for so you must add forty Dollars
to the above

An invoice, made out in 1835, for the sale of ten Negroes—eleven including "Nancy child," whom the owner reluctantly sold for an additional forty dollars because the child's mother "made such a damned fuss I had to let her take it."

CHAPTER THREE

SLAVERY AND

ABOLITIONISM

By 1850, there were more than three million slaves in fifteen southern states. To many southerners of the 1850's, slavery seemed as much a part of their heritage as their language, their customs, and their cotton fields. In the fifteen northern states, slavery was prohibited by law. To most northerners and westerners, slavery was the South's "peculiar institution," something alien to their own social and economic practices. Yet the presence of slavery in America affected the entire nation. It had been debated, protested, defended, compromised, and fought over since the union of the states in 1789, and it would come close to destroying that union in the 1860's. It affected American society so profoundly that today, more than a hundred years after the abolition of slavery in the United States, we are still struggling with the problems it created.

The Origins of Slavery in the United States

Slavery was not an American invention. It had existed in Europe, Asia, and Africa since the time of the pharaohs, and before. Arriving with the earliest Spanish and Portugese explorers, slavery was eventually practiced throughout the New World, in one form or another, by all of the major colonial powers. Indians were used as slave labor in many parts of Central and South America; in other places, where

The slave deck of the bark *Wildfire* at Key West, Florida, 1860. Although the United States was officially closed to the slave trade in 1808, many shiploads of foreign Negroes were successfully smuggled into the South after that date.

the Indian population was sparse or could not be dominated easily, people were brought from Europe and Africa to work the land. The use of African labor proved particularly profitable on the British, French, Dutch, and Spanish sugar plantations of the Caribbean—the demand for their sugar and molasses was worldwide, and their demand for labor, in turn, made the slave trade big business during the seventeenth and eighteenth centuries. In the eighteenth century, it is estimated that from 50,000 to 100,000 Africans were taken from their homes and shipped across the Atlantic every year, most of them bound for the slave markets of the West Indies and Brazil.

Slavery developed rather slowly in the colonies along the Atlantic seaboard of North America. Negroes came first, slavery as an institution took form afterwards, and laws protecting it came still later. It has often been assumed that slavery began in Virginia in 1619. That date, however, simply marked the introduction of a new racial element into an English settlement. Brought by a Dutch ship and sold to Jamestown residents, the twenty Negro arrivals, as Ulrich Phillips pointed out, "were not fully slaves in the hands of their Virginia buyers, for there was neither law nor custom then establishing the institution of slavery in the colony."[1] They were instead considered indentured servants, in common with a number of Caucasian inhabitants. An indentured servant was bound by custom and law to work for somebody else, often the person who had paid his passage to America, for a specified period of time. When the time was up, he became again his own master. Indentured servitude was instituted after several early attempts to use Indian labor had failed—manpower was needed to work the Virginia land for its increasingly profitable export crop, tobacco. Indentured servitude did not turn into slavery. Slavery developed as a separate institution, and it was applied only to blacks.

During their early years in Virginia, as in the other colonies, Negroes apparently lived and worked among the white settlers without suffering from discrimination based on color. Like white indentured servants, they worked out their terms of servitude, acquired land, married and raised families, and even bought indentured servants of their own. They were able to vote and testify in court and to mingle

[1] Ulrich B. Phillips, *American Negro Slavery* (New York: D. Appleton & Co., 1918), p. 75.

freely with whites. According to Lerone Bennett, Jr.,

The racial situation, at this juncture, was fluid; it contained the seeds of several alternatives. Indentured servitude could have continued for black and white servants or both groups could have been reduced to slavery. Other possibilities were Indian slavery and a free labor system for blacks and whites, Indians and immigrants. Socioeconomic forces selected black slavery out of these alternatives. In the West Indies, sugar was decisive. In America, tobacco and cotton were the villains. A world-wide demand for these products and the rise of plantation-sized units to meet this demand focused attention on the labor force. How could men be *forced* to work?

The rulers of the early American colonies were not overly scrupulous about the color or national origin of their work force. Indian slavery was tried and abandoned. Many masters attempted to enslave white men and women. When these attempts failed, the spotlight fell on the African. He was tried and he was not found wanting. Why were Africans more acceptable than poor whites and poor Indians? White men, for one thing, were under the protection of strong governments; they could appeal to a monarch. White men, moreover, were white; they could escape and blend into the crowd. Indians, too, could escape; they knew the country and their brothers were only a hill or a forest away. Another element in the failure of Indian slavery was the fact that Indians tended to sicken and die.

Africans did not have these disadvantages. They were strong; one African, the Spanish said, was worth four Indians. They were inexpensive: the same money that would buy an Irish or English indentured servant for ten years would buy an African for life. They were visible: they could run, but they could not blend into the crowd. Above all, they were unprotected. And the supply, unlike the supply of Irishmen and Englishmen, seemed to be inexhaustible. The rulers of early America fell to thinking. Why not?

Virginia and Maryland led the way in the 1660's. Laws made Africans servants for life; intermarriage was forbidden; children born of African women were ruled bond or free, according to the status of the mother.

At first, religion was the rationalization; Africans were good material for slavery because they were not Christians. Between 1667 and 1682, the basis shifted to race. Virginia said it first, in her law of 1667: " . . . the conferring of baptisme doth not alter the condition of the person as to his bondage or freedom." After that, it was easy. A series of laws stripped the black slave of all rights of personalty and made color a badge of servitude. The black population, which had grown slowly during the twilight interim of freedom, lunged forward. By 1710, the number had increased to 50,000. When the Declaration of Independence was signed, there were 500,000. . . .[2]

Slavery was practiced in all of the colonies until the American Revolution, although the number of slaves and the treatment they received varied from colony to colony. In New England in 1776 only one out of fifty inhabitants was black; slaves were not a significant part of the labor force. The slave trade itself, however, had made wealthy men of many northern merchants, and the region's profitable sugar, molasses, and rum trade, its shipbuilding industry, and its distilleries were to a large extent dependent on the traffic in slaves. Despite the importance of slavery to their economy, many New Englanders opposed the institution—some on religious grounds, others because it violated the growing spirit of democratic idealism that was to be expressed by Thomas Jefferson in the Declaration of Independence. On the whole, slaves were treated more moderately in New England than in the other colonies. Although they were owned as property, they also had some rights as persons—they could marry, they could testify in court, and they had the right to a trial by jury.

Caesar, a former New York house slave, photographed in 1850.

Slaves made up a larger part of the labor force in the Middle Atlantic colonies than in New England, but there too attitudes toward slavery were mixed. The earliest recorded formal protest against slavery in the colonies had come from a group of Pennsylvania Quakers in 1688. Both Alexander Hamilton of New York and Benjamin Franklin

[2]Lerone Bennett, Jr., *Before the Mayflower: A History of Black America,* rev. ed. (Chicago: Johnson Publishing Co., 1969), pp. 36–38. Copyright © 1969 by Johnson Publishing Company, Inc.

Library of Congress

A slave auction, 1861. Professional traders bought surplus slaves from tobacco planters in the Upper South and sold them to cotton planters in the Deep South.

of Pennsylvania were leaders of abolitionist societies when they attended the Constitutional Convention in 1787.

By 1787, six states—Vermont, Massachusetts, New Hampshire, Pennsylvania, Connecticut, and Rhode Island —had either abolished slavery outright or had provided for gradual abolition. New Jersey would follow in 1804 and New York in 1827. Many northern delegates to the Constitutional Convention, and some southerners as well, hoped that slavery would be abolished in all the states under the new federal government. But a substantial number of southern delegates were determined that it should not be. According to James Madison, "the most material difference" among the delegates was "principally from their having or not having slaves." The issue was strong enough to threaten the unity of the states, and in the end the antislavery forces compromised. Article I, Section 2 of the newly drafted Constitution allowed the slave states to count three-fifths of their slaves in determining how many representa-

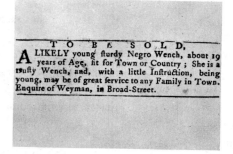

TO BE SOLD,

A Likely negro Man, his Wife and Child; the negro Man capable of doing all forts of Plantation Work, and a good Miller: The Woman exceeding fit for a Farmer, being capable of doing any Work, belonging to a Houfe in the Country, at reafonable Rates, inquire of the Printer hereof.

TO BE SOLD,

A LIKELY young fturdy Negro Wench, about 19 years of Age, fit for Town or Country; She is a trufty Wench, and, with a little Inftruction, being young, may be of great fervice to any Family in Town. Enquire of Weyman, in Broad-Street.

tives they would elect to Congress; Article IV, Section 2 provided that the free states must return any fugitive slaves to their owners in the slave states; and Article II, Section 9, permitted the importation of slaves into the United States until 1807, another twenty years.

For while slavery had died out in the North, it had flourished in the South. At the time of the Revolution, two out of three South Carolinians were black. Slaves *were* the labor force of the South, the foundation of its economy and the cornerstone of its culture. But why the institution took root there so deeply is a question that historians have not yet resolved.

Some historians have suggested that the humid, subtropical climate determined the nature of southern institutions and the structure of southern society. Southerners, in permitting slavery to grow, merely submitted to compelling natural factors that included soil, topography, and climate. Although an opponent of the climate, or environmental, theory, Kenneth Stampp has provided an excellent description of the idea:

> . . . Combine the hot summers and long growing seasons with the rich southern soils—the alluvial river bottoms, the sandy loams of the coastal plains, the silt loams of the Black Belt, and the red clays of the piedmont—and an agricultural economy was the logical result. Add the many navigable rivers which facilitated the movement of bulky staples from considerable distances inland to coastal ports, and all the requirements for a commercial form of agriculture were at hand. Commercial agriculture induced a

trend toward large landholdings which in turn created a demand for labor.[3]

Historians who oppose the environmental theory argue that the same natural conditions have produced vastly different human responses. In the American Southwest, for example, within a hundred-mile radius, some Indian tribes were nomadic hunters, others were sedentary farmers, some were involved in commercial activities, while still other tribes were grouped together, urban fashion, in cliff dwellings—one environment, but a variety of social and economic responses. Reasoning from this evidence, it does not follow that the only response to the southern environment was a plantation system using slave labor. Nor does it follow that the plantation system required the use of slaves. Historians have pointed out that the plantation system was older than slavery and survived its abolition, suggesting that slavery did not play a role in the economic structure of the system that could not have been filled in some other way.

In the early 1800's many people believed, and many historians since have agreed, that slavery might have died out gradually in the South had it not been for Eli Whitney's invention of the cotton gin in 1793. The heart of the cotton plant, the boll, is a tangle of fibers and seeds. Whitney's ginning machine could separate the seeds from the fibers rapidly. Working only with his hands, one man was able to separate a mere pound of cotton fiber a day. With a gin, even operating it by hand, one man could separate fifty pounds of cotton a day. When water or steam power was applied to the machine, one man could produce more than a thousand pounds of seedless cotton a day. The cotton gin, together with the newly invented power spinning and weaving machines operating in England and the northern United States, made commercial cotton growing a highly profitable enterprise.

The result was a tremendous expansion in southern cotton growing. In 1791 the total American production of cotton fiber had been only 400 bales. By 1810 it had risen

[3] Kenneth Stampp, *The Peculiar Institution* (New York: Alfred A. Knopf, 1956), p. 4.

to 171,000 bales. By 1830 it had climbed to 731,000 bales, and in 1860 the figure was over 5,000,000 bales or two-thirds of the world's total production of cotton.

In order to clear the land and to plant and pick cotton, a large supply of inexpensive labor was needed. For this cotton planters relied on slave labor and believed they had no choice. The number of slaves in the South rose from approximately one million in 1800 to about four million in 1860.

Although most historians agree that the rise of large-scale commercial cotton growing had a profound influence on the development of slavery in the United States, some believe that the institution would have survived in the South even if the cotton gin had never been invented. These historians maintain that slavery was not dying out in the South before 1793, and they suggest that the institution was more deeply rooted in southern attitudes toward race than in economics. Cotton simply provided southerners with a strong economic motive for perpetuating an institution that they supported for social and cultural reasons. Nor can cotton alone be held responsible for the dramatic increase in the number of slaves in the South from 1800 to 1860, for the bulk of the increase occurred after 1808, when the United States was closed to the international slave trade by an act of the federal government. Most of the slaves who became part of the southern plantation system after 1800 were native-born Americans.

In 1860, the South's four million slaves engaged in a wide variety of occupations. Many worked in the homes of the planters. Some women learned to spin, weave, and sew; others became cooks, maids, laundresses, dairymaids, and nurses. Men became blacksmiths, painters, and shoemakers, while a few learned carpentry and bricklaying. The great majority of the slaves on cotton, rice, and sugar-cane plantations, however, were laborers who worked in the fields. They planted cotton, corn, and wheat in the spring; cultivated the crops in the summer; picked cotton, harvested grain, and slaughtered livestock in the fall; and mended fences and cleared new land in the winter.

The lack of adequate records makes it difficult to generalize on the treatment of slaves. Generally speaking, there is evidence that slaves on the small plantations and farms were more humanely treated than those on the large plantations. Yet there is also some evidence indicating that slaves on the large plantations of the lower South had more food, better quarters, and superior medical care than those belonging to small owners.

On large plantations the slaves usually worked in gangs under the general management of a white overseer, and the more specific control of a black driver, an unusually intelligent and able slave selected from the group. Treatment given the slaves on plantations where an overseer was in charge was likely to be severe, probably because overseers did not have the personal investment in slaves that the owners had. Many planters may have treated their slaves well because they considered them valuable property. A planter who owned fifty able-bodied slaves during the 1850's had an investment of at least $50,000. The death of a single slave represented a substantial loss, and sickness or injury from ill-treatment was contrary to a planter's best interests. To protect his investments he generally tried to keep his slaves adequately fed, clothed, and housed. Certainly this would seem to make economic sense, but exactly how many slaveowners actually felt this way is impossible to say.

Historical Views of the Slave System

Like its origins, the merits and evils of the slave system have long been a subject of controversy and they continue to be debated. A scholarly indictment of the system came from the nineteenth-century historian, James Ford Rhodes. He described the system as intrinsically corrupt, breeding injustice, oppression, and brutality. Rhodes attacked the assertion that antebellum slaves were better housed, clothed, and fed than laborers in northern cities, and he cited evidence to show that they were frequently overworked to the point of physical exhaustion. He described their utter lack of legal protection, and showed how the domestic slave trade—which separated husbands from wives and parents from children—destroyed whatever family life a slave might

The New York Historical Society

Newly freed slaves on a southern plantation, 1862.

have had. Rhodes pictured the slave's helplessness against the aggressions of brutal masters, as exemplified by the numerous transactions involving the use of mulatto and quadroon girls as prostitutes. He emphasized the slave's degraded condition and his constant longing for freedom, and in so doing Rhodes established a pattern of writing on American Negro slavery that remained the standard for twenty years.

In 1918, Ulrich B. Phillips published his *American Negro Slavery.* Unlike Rhodes, Phillips considered slavery a benign and patriarchal institution, within which such virtues as mutual loyalty and gentleness flourished. Drawing from plantation records, he attacked Rhodes' generalizations about inadequate food, clothing, and housing. He also asserted that stories of cruelty and overwork were exaggerated. Phillips emphasized the serene nature of the plantation regime, and the warm human relationship between master and blacks. He admitted that there were instances of injustice and oppression, but implied that these were overbalanced by gentleness, kind-hearted friendship, and mutual loyalty and dependence. "On the whole," Phillips wrote,

> . . . the plantations were the best schools yet invented for the mass training of that sort of inert and backward people which the bulk of the American negroes represented. The lack of any regular provision for the discharge of the pupils upon the completion of their training was, of course, a cardinal shortcoming which the laws of slavery imposed; but even in view of this, the slavery plantation regime, after having wrought the initial and irreparable misfortune of causing the negroes to be imported, did at least as much as any system possible in the period could have done toward adapting the bulk of them to life in a civilized community.[4]

A slave nurse, or "mammy," about 1860.

One recent evaluation of American slavery is found in *Time on the Cross*, a controversial work by Robert Fogel and Stanley Engerman. Some historians have hailed *Time on the Cross* as one of the most important books of the decade, while others charge that it is seriously flawed by misinterpretations of quantitative evidence. *Time on the Cross* offers startling new conclusions that contradict most established views. Among Fogel and Engerman's assertions are the following:

1. Slavery was not a system irrationally kept in existence by plantation owners who failed to perceive or were indifferent to their best economic interests. The purchase of a slave was generally a highly profitable investment which yielded rates of return that compared favorably with the most outstanding investment opportunities in manufacturing.

2. The slave system was not economically moribund on the eve of the Civil War. There is no evidence that economic forces alone would have soon brought slavery to an end without the necessity of a war or some other form of political intervention. Quite the contrary, as the Civil War approached, slavery as an economic system was never stronger and the trend was toward even further entrenchment.

[4] Phillips, *Negro Slavery*, p. 343.

3. Slaveowners were not becoming pessimistic about the future of their system during the decade that preceded the Civil War. The rise of the secessionist movement coincided with a wave of optimism. On the eve of the Civil War, slaveholders anticipated an era of unprecedented prosperity.

4. Slave agriculture was not inefficient compared with free agriculture. Economics of large-scale operation, effective management, and intensive utilization of labor and capital made southern slave agriculture 35 percent more efficient than the northern system of family farming.

5. The typical slave field hand was not lazy, inept, and unproductive. On the average he was harder-working and more efficient than his white counterpart.

6. The course of slavery in the cities does not prove that slavery was incompatible with an industrial system or that slaves were unable to cope with an industrial regimen. Slaves employed in industry compared favorably with free workers in diligence and efficiency. Far from declining, the demand for slaves was actually increasing more rapidly in urban areas than in the countryside.

7. The belief that slave-breeding, sexual exploitation, and promiscuity destroyed the black family is a myth. The family was the basic unit of social organization under slavery. It was to the economic interest of planters to encourage the stability of slave families and most of them did so. Most slave sales were either of whole families or of individuals who were at an age when it would have been normal for them to have left the family.

8. The material (not psychological) conditions of the lives of slaves compared favorably with those of free industrial workers. This is not to say that they were good by modern standards. It merely emphasizes the hard lot of all workers, free or slave, during the first half of the nineteenth century.

9. Slaves were exploited in the sense that part of the income which they produced was expropriated by their

owners. However, the rate of expropriation was much lower than has generally been presumed. Over the course of his lifetime, the typical slave field hand received about 90 percent of the income he produced.

10. Far from stagnating, the economy of the antebellum South grew quite rapidly. Between 1840 and 1860, per capita income increased more rapidly in the South than in the rest of the nation. By 1860 the South attained a level of per capita income which was high by the standards of the time.[5]

The ten conclusions above represent only a partial list of the modified views with which Fogel and Engerman contradict many of the long-held, traditional assumptions regarding the economics of slavery in the ante-bellum South. *Time on the Cross* should be read with care. It should be read with the knowledge that some of the conclusions are supported weakly and that others are drawn from data related only to a Louisiana sugar plantation, which is much too narrow a base on which to found sweeping generalizations for the total southern slave enterprise. Nonetheless, the work is an important contribution to the literature on slavery and cannot be ignored.

Negro Views of Slavery

What about the slaves themselves? What did they think of the system? Many reminiscences of slaves and former slaves exist. They do not display a uniform attitude toward the institution.

A Favorable View

Was born in 1849, but I don't know just when. My birthday comes in fodder-pulling time 'cause my ma said she was pulling up til 'bout an hour 'fore I was born. Was born in North Carolina and was a young lady at the time of surrender.

[5] Robert William Fogel and Stanley L. Engerman, *Time on the Cross: The Economics of American Negro Slavery* (Boston: Little, Brown, 1974), pp. 4–6. Copyright © 1974 by Little, Brown and Company, Inc. Reprinted by permission of Little, Brown and Company.

I don't 'member Old Master's name; all I 'member is that we call 'em Old Master and Old Mistress. They had 'bout a hundred niggers, and they was rich. Master always tended the men, and Mistress tended to us.

And we had plenty to eat. Whooo-ee! Just plenty to eat. Old Master's folks raised plenty of meat, and they raise their sugar, rice, peas, chickens, eggs, cows, and just everything good to eat.

Every evening at three 'clock Old Mistress would call all us litsy bitsy children in, and we would lay down on pallets and have to go to sleep. I can hear her now singing to us pickaninnies. . . .

When I got big 'nough I nursed my mistress' baby. When the baby go to sleep in the evening, I would put it in the cradly and lay down by the cradly and go to sleep. I played a heap while I was little. We played Susanna Gal, jump rope, calling cows, running, jumping, skipping, and just everything we could think of. When I got big 'nough to cook, I cooked then.

The kitchen of the big house was built 'way off from the house, and we cooked on a great big old fireplace. We had swing pots and would swing 'em over the fire and cook and had a big old skillet with legs on it. We call it a oven and cooked bread and cakes in it.

We had the best mistress and master in the world, and they was Christian folks, and taught us to be Christian-like too. Every Sunday morning Old Master would have all us niggers to the house while he would sing and pray and read the Bible to us all. Old Master taught us not to be bad; he taught us to be good; he told us to never steal nor to tell false tales and not to do anything that was bad. He said: "You will reap what you sow, that you sow it single and reap double." I learnt that when I was a little child, and I ain't forgot it yet. When I got grown I went the Baptist way. God called my pa to preach and Old Master let him preach in the kitchen and in the back yard under the trees. On preaching day Old Master took his whole family and all the slaves to church with him.

We had log schoolhouses in them days, and folks learnt more than they does in the bricks today.

Down in the quarters every black family had a one- or two-room log cabin. We didn't have no floors in them cabins. Nice dirt floors was the style then, and we used sage brooms. Took a string and tied the sage together and had a nice broom outen that. We would gather broom sage for our winter brooms just like we gathered our other winter stuff. We kept dirt floors swept as clean and white. And our bed was big and tall and had little beds to push under there. They was all little enough to go under the other and in the daytime we would push 'em all under the big one and make heaps of room. Our beds was stuffed with hay and straw and shucks, and, believe me, child, they sure slept good.

Now, child, I can't 'member everything I done in them days, but we didn't have to worry 'bout nothing. Old Mistress was the one to worry. 'Twasn't then like it is now, no 'twasn't. We had such a good time, and everybody cried when the Yankees cried out: "Free." T'other niggers say they had a hard time 'fore they was free, but 'twas then like 'tis now. If you had a hard time, we done it ourselves.

Old Master didn't want to part with his niggers, and the niggers didn't want to part with Old Master, so they thought by coming to Arkansas they would have a chance to keep 'em. So they got on their way. We loaded up our wagons and put up our wagon sheet, and we had plenty to eat and plenty of horse feed. We traveled 'bout fifteen or twenty miles a day and would stop and camp at night. We would cook enough in the morning to last all day. The cows was drove together. Some was gentle and some was not, and did they have a time. I mean, they *had* a time. While we was on our way, Old Master died, and three of the slaves died too. We buried the slaves there, but we camped while Old Master was carried back to North Carolina. When Old Mistress come back, we started on to Arkansas and reached here safe, but when we got here we found freedom too. Old Mistress begged us to stay with her, and we stayed till she died, then they took her back to Carolina. There wasn't nobody left but Miss Nancy, and she soon married and left, and I lost track of her and Mr. Tom.[6]

[6] Benjamin A. Botkin, ed., *Lay My Burden Down: A Folk History of Slavery* (Chicago: University of Chicago Press, 1961), pp. 61–62.

An Unfavorable View

We wore chains all the time. When we work, we drug them chains with us. At night he lock us to a tree to keep us from running off. He didn't have to do that. We were 'fraid to run. We knew he'd kill us. Besides, he brands us, and they no way to git it off. It's put there with a hot iron. You can't git it off.

If a slave die, Massa made the rest of us tie a rope round he feet and drag him off. Never buried one, it was too much trouble. . . .

I seen children sold off and the mammy not sold, and sometimes the mammy sold and a little baby kept on the place and give to another woman to raise. Them white folks didn't care nothing 'bout how the slaves grieved when they tore up a family.

Old Man Saunders was the hardest overseer of anybody. He would git mad and give a whipping sometime, and the slave wouldn't even know what it was about.

My uncle Sandy was the lead row nigger, and he was a good nigger and never would touch a drap of liquor. One night some the niggers git hold of some liquor somehow, and they leave the jug half full on the step of Sandy's cabin. Next morning Old Man Saunders come out in the field so mad he was pale.

A planter and his overseer.

He just go to the lead row and tell Sandy to go with him and start toward the woods along Bois d'Arc Creek, with Sandy following behind. The overseer always carry a big heavy stick, but we didn't know he was so mad, and they just went off in the woods.

Pretty soon we hear Sandy hollering, and we know old overseer pouring it on, then the overseer come back by hisself and go on up to the house.

Come late evening he come and see what we done in the day's work, and go back to the quarters with us all. When he git to Mammy's cabin, where Grandmammy live too, he say to Grandmammy, "I sent Sandy down in the woods to hunt a hoss, he gwine come in hungry pretty soon. You better make him a extra hoecake," and he kind of laugh and go on to his house.

Just soon as he gone, we tell Grandmammy we think he got a whipping, and sure 'nough he didn't come in.

The next day some white boys finds Uncle Sandy where that overseer done killed him and throwed him in a little pond, and they never done nothing to Old Man Saunders at all!

When he go to whip a nigger he make him strip to the waist, and he take a cat-o'-nine-tails and bring the blisters with a wide strap of leather fastened to a stick handle. I seen the blood running outen many a back, all the way from the neck to the waist!

Many the time a nigger git blistered and cut up so that we have to git a sheet and grease it with lard and wrap 'em up in it, and they have to wear a greasy cloth around they body under the shirt for three-four days after they git a big whipping![7]

Slave quarters on a South Carolina plantation, 1860.

A View of the Free Negro

Slavery time was tough, boss. You just don't know how tough it was. I can't 'splain to you just how bad all the niggers want to get they freedom. With the free niggers it was just the same as it was with them that was in bondage. You know there was some few free niggers in that time even 'fore the slaves taken outen bondage. It was really worse on them than it was with them what wasn't free. The slaveowners, they just despised them free niggers and make it just as hard on them as they can. They couldn't get no work from nobody. Wouldn't nary man hire 'em or give 'em any work at all. So because they was up against it and never had any money or nothing, the white folks make these free niggers 'sess the taxes. And 'cause they never had no money for to pay the tax with, they was put up on the block by the court man or the sheriff and sold out to somebody for enough to pay the tax what they say they owe. So they keep these free niggers hired out all the time 'most, working for to pay the taxes. I 'member one of them free niggers mighty well. He was called Free Sol. He had him a little home and a old woman and some boys. They was kept bounded out nigh 'bout all the time working for to pay they tax. Yes, sir, boss, it was heap more better to be a slave nigger than

[7] Ibid., pp. 76, 106.

a free one. And it was really a heavenly day when the freedom come for the race.[8]

Slave Rebellions

Individual slaves resisted slavery by running away. Altogether, the South may have lost as many as 100,000 slaves in this way, but this is only a guess. Some Negroes organized revolts, but none came anywhere near success.

In 1800 Gabriel Prosser carefully planned an assault on Richmond, Virginia. For months he studied the layout of the streets and plotted the strategy by which he and his men would seize the town's arsenal. On August 30, Prosser and his men marched, armed with a few guns but mainly with scythes and pikes. But two slaves had betrayed the plan to the governor. He had called out the militia and Prosser's rebellion was crushed. Thirty-five Negroes were executed as a result.

Harriet Tubman was an escaped slave who led over three hundred slaves north to freedom. During the Civil War she served as a nurse and later as a scout for the Union Army.

A rebellion in South Carolina in 1822 was also quickly put down as a result of betrayal. Denmark Vesey, a free Negro, planned to capture Charleston and kill all the whites, but this plot failed before the slaves could take action.

Of all the recorded slave revolts, Nat Turner's in Virginia in 1831 was the bloodiest. By the time he was thirty years old Turner had been owned by several men, had learned to read and write, and had become a Baptist preacher. A mystic, Turner often fasted and prayed for long periods of time and frequently heard voices and saw visions. He came to believe that he had been chosen by God to rid the nation of slavery.

On the night of August 21, 1831, Turner and six fellow slaves stole into the house of planter Joseph Travis. They killed the entire family. Gathering about sixty-five other slaves, the band moved from plantation to plantation, leaving blood and death as they went. Within two days they had killed sixty white men, women, and children.

Whites then struck back. Militia and vigilante groups converged on Turner and his band and killed or captured all but Turner himself. He was finally taken near the Travis

[8] Ibid., pp. 73–74.

house on October 30. Tried and convicted, Turner was hanged less than a month later.

Nat Turner's rebellion sent a shock of horror and fear through the South. People, one woman wrote to a friend,

> lie down to sleep with fear. They hardly venture out on nights. A lady told me, that for weeks after the tragedy, she had quivered at every blast of wind, and every blow of the shutter. Bolts and bars were tied, but the horrid fear haunted the entire population day and night.

"Nat Turner and His Confederates in Conference," an 1863 engraving. Nat Turner's revolt sent a shock of terror throughout the South.

Some southerners panicked, and shot or hanged slaves even vaguely rumored to harbor ideas of rebellion. During the next few years whites who expressed antislavery views, or who were suspected of holding such views, were driven from the South. Antislavery literature was publicly burned, and some southern postmasters destroyed it instead of delivering it. Southerners by now had committed themselves and their section irrevocably to slavery. If they any longer bothered to defend it at all, it was as a positive good.

Fear of rebellion also prompted the southern states to pass new legislation strengthening their slave codes, and to enforce existing code provisions more strictly. The slave codes, which dated from colonial times, imposed severe and detailed restrictions on the movement and conduct of slaves. For example, slaves were prohibited from marrying legally, from learning to read and write, and from traveling beyond the limits of their plantations. The codes also provided harsh penalties for slaves who violated such restrictions— running away might be punishable by death.

Slave Life

It is common knowledge that blacks resisted slavery by breaking tools, shirking, and feigning illness as well as by outright rebellion and running away, and there may have been other, more subtle kinds of resistance. Through the development of their own culture, Negroes may have achieved some degree of autonomy within the confines of the white plantation-oriented culture. In a 1970 essay and in *Roll, Jordan, Roll*, Eugene D. Genovese has suggested that historians might gain a clear perspective on slavery and perhaps find clues pointing to the development of a separate culture by paying more attention to what went on in slave quarters. They might, he thinks, give more consideration to the relationships among slaves and their relationships to whites on the plantation:

> We have made a grave error in the way in which we have viewed slave life, and this error has been perpetuated by both whites and blacks, racists and anti-racists. The traditional proslavery view and that of such later apologists for white supremacy as Ulrich B. Phillips have treated the blacks as objects of white benevolence and fear—as people who needed both protection and control—and devoted attention to the ways in which black slaves adjusted to the demands of the master class. Abolitionist propaganda and the later and now dominant liberal viewpoint have insisted that the slave regime was so brutal and dehumanizing that blacks should be seen primarily as victims. Both these viewpoints treat black people almost wholly as objects, never as creative participants in a social process, never as half of a two-part subject.[9]

To Genovese an important question is not so much what was done to the slaves, but rather, what did they do for themselves and how did they do it? He further believes that many conclusions that have been reached concerning slave religion and family life, and the roles of house slaves and drivers, have been based on sketchy evidence and to a large extent on legend.

Slaves may have developed a separate and distinct religion as one means of achieving a certain amount of cultural autonomy. Although there is insufficient evidence to warrant definitive judgments on the question, Genovese

Slaves received a weekly ration of food—usually corn meal, bacon, salt, and molasses. The planter also supplied some tools and utensils, and clothing.

[9] Eugene D. Genovese, "American Slaves and Their History," *The New York Review of Books* 15, no. 10 (December 3, 1970): 34. Reprinted with permission from *The New York Review of Books.* Copyright © 1970, NYREV, Inc.

suggests that by combining elements of African religions and Christianity, slaves forged not only an instrument for autonomy but also one for resistance to whites. Slaves did adopt Christianity. At the same time, however, evidence indicates that every plantation had its conjurer, voodoo man, or witch doctor. It is possible, Genovese contends,

> that a distinctly black religion, at least in embryo, appeared in the slave quarters and played a role in shaping the daily lives of the slaves. In other words, quite apart from the problem of religion as a factor in overt resistance to slavery, we need to know how the slaves developed a religious life that enabled them to survive as autonomous human beings with a culture of their own within the white master's world.[10]

What about family life among the slaves? What we believe about it may be based more on legend than on fact. It is true that slave marriages were not given legal recognition in the southern states. Yet, Genovese points out, the slave population increased in rough proportion to the white population. The external slave trade could not account for this; the slave trade ended in 1808 and the smuggling which occurred after that date did not bring a significantly large number of Negroes into the country. Abolitionists contended that slave-breeding farms in Maryland and Virginia did much to increase the black population. Genovese, however, finds little evidence that there was slave breeding on a significant scale. The exportation of slaves from Maryland and Virginia could have resulted as an attempt to drain off the natural increase and to supplement a decreasing income from agriculture. In those two states tobacco had long been the principal crop, and it was one of diminishing returns owing to its tendency to drain minerals from the soil. There must have been, Genovese suggests, some kind of sanction, however illegal, given to slave marriages and family life. Plantation life, after all, was commonly organized by family units. And it would seem economically advantageous to owners to provide at least minimum satisfaction to slaves in the way of food, living space, and recreational time to

[10] Ibid., p. 35.

Library of Congress

A slave family
representing five
generations, all born
on the Smith
plantation near
Beaufort, South
Carolina.

reinforce family life. Such a policy would benefit morale
and would probably get more work out of slaves than would
a contrary policy. The important thing, says Genovese,

> is that the prevailing standard of decency was not easily
> violated because the slaves had come to understand their
> own position. If a master wished to keep his plantation
> going, he had to learn the limits of his slaves' endurance.
> If, for example, he decided to ignore the prevailing custom
> of giving Sundays off or of giving an extended Christmas
> holiday, his slaves would feel sorely tried and would cer-
> tainly pay him back with one or another form of destruc-
> tion. The slaves remained in a weak position, but they were
> rarely completely helpless, and by guile, brute courage, and
> a variety of other devices they taught every master just
> where the line was he dared not cross if he wanted a crop.
> In precisely this way, slaves took up the masters' interest in
> their family life and turned it to account. The typical
> plantation in the Upper South and the Lower was organized
> by family units. Man and wife lived together with children,
> and to a considerable degree the man was in fact the man
> in the house.[11]

[11] Ibid., p. 36.

Certain white practices, of course, mitigated against a stable slave family life, particularly sales that broke up families, and violations of individual black women. No one today can view these practices as anything but unjust, immoral, and reprehensible. They alone are sufficient grounds to condemn the whole system of slavery. Yet what effects did they have on the family life of those forced to live in slavery? No one knows with any certainty. Sources indicate that despite these practices,

> the average plantation slave lived in a family setting, developed strong family ties, and held the nuclear family as the proper social norm. It is true that planters who often had to excuse others, or even themselves, for breaking up families by sale, would sometimes argue that blacks did not really form deep and lasting attachments, that they lacked a strong family sense, that they were naturally promiscuous, and so forth. Abolitionists and former slaves would reinforce the prevalent notion by saying that slavery was so horrible no real family tie could be maintained. Since planters, abolitionists, and former slaves all said the same thing, it has usually been taken as the truth. Only it was not.[12]

The sources, Genovese points out, say all these things, but just as frequently they say the opposite. Planters often agonized over breaking up families, for whatever reason, and they seemed to encourage slaves to live in family units, if for no other reason than a man with a wife and children to worry about was usually easier to control. Among the slaves themselves there was as wide a variety of behavior as might be found among any group of people. Some men spent a lifetime with the same woman; the behavior of others bordered on polygamy. Some were promiscuous; others were not. Some upheld standards of sexual morality similar to those of whites; others adhered to different standards. Yet, Genovese contends, family life seems to have been the accepted norm, and thousands of blacks spent many Reconstruction years searching for lost wives, husbands, or children. "The experience of slaves," he concludes, "for all its tragic disruptions, pointed toward a

[12] Ibid.

stable postslavery family life, and recent scholarship demonstrates conclusively that the reconstruction and postreconstruction black experience carried forward the acceptance of the nuclear-family norm."[13]

With respect to the role of the man in family life, it has frequently been asserted that as a chattel subject always to the power of the white master, the Negro male was unable to carry out normal functions as the head of a family. He could not protect his woman, fully control his children, or act as the real breadwinner. Slavery emasculated the Negro male and, as a result, black women held him in contempt.

There is truth in this. But, says Genovese, there were cases—however exceptional—in which plantation owners understood that before they could punish certain slave women they would have to kill their men first. And it is possible that some women, at least, did not expect the impossible from their men. Far from being contemptuous, they gave their love and support within the restrictions imposed by slave life.

Negro men, Genovese points out, often supplemented the family diet by hunting and trapping. They divided the labor of caring for the family garden with their wives and they shared authority over the children with them. Although it is fragmentary, evidence for this is found in slave narratives, and the evidence suggests that even under deplorable conditions Negro men asserted themselves as best they could, and that probably many Negro men and women achieved and maintained some sense of dignity and autonomy. Negro women, Genovese thinks, should be praised not only for doing much to help hold families together, but also for supporting their men and helping them resist emasculation and dehumanization. Without such support, few black men could have survived the system.

What was the relationship of house slaves to their masters and to their fellow Negroes? Genovese suggests that they may not have been the simple Uncle Toms they have often been portrayed as being. They must have been more complicated human beings than that.

In many instances, house slaves constituted a separate

[13] Ibid., p. 37.

Slaves harvesting sugar cane on a Louisiana plantation. Slave labor was also used in the sugar mill shown at the left of the drawing.

and privileged class of slaves. Yet their lives must have been extremely ambivalent. They had to share intimately the life of the planter family, and they tended to take on white behavior with respect to dress, manners, religion, and prejudice. Some were informers; it was house slaves who tipped off whites about Denmark Vesey's plans for revolt in South Carolina in 1822. Much evidence has been cited to show that house slaves believed that white interests were their interests and that they considered themselves above and better than field hands.

There is another side to the picture, however. House slaves were no less slaves than the others. They were subject to similar restraints and were punished with whippings and deprivation of privileges. "It is impossible," writes Genovese, "to think of people, black and white, slave and master, thrown together in the intimacy of the Big House without realizing that they had to emerge loving and hating each other." And he points out that in many cases house slaves had to spend part of the time in slave quarters, espe-

cially on the many small plantations where there were relatively few slaves. Under such circumstances it would hardly
pay them to put on airs. Many house slaves ran away.
Often those who looked and acted the most docile proved
the most rebellious. While some remained on the plantation
and helped protect it and the family during the war years,
a good many others were among the first to leave and find
protection behind Union lines. There is abundant evidence
in planters' letters and diaries that they were shocked and
surprised at the defection of house slaves. This indicates
that many whites did not really know the blacks with whom
they associated in an informal way day in and day out,
and whom they thought they had treated with especial kindness and consideration.

Drivers—black slave foremen—have also been mis-
understood, Genovese believes. These men were selected
by owners on the basis of their intelligence, strength, and
leadership qualities. They worked directly under the master
or his white overseer and were directly responsible for many
of the details of operating a plantation. "In the existing
literature," Genovese says, "the drivers appear as ogres,
monsters, betrayers, and sadists." Some undoubtedly were.
Others, perhaps, were not.

Drivers were in an odd position. They had to follow
white orders and they had to see that the work was done.
Frequently they had to punish other slaves. Yet they were
slaves too. Although they represented the master in the
slave quarters, they also represented the slaves to the
master. They were the masters' check on their overseers,
many of whom were brutal and incompetent, and while
overseers came and went, drivers remained. It is likely that
many drivers led the workers instead of pushing them, and
that they did what they could to soften punishments and
generally protect their fellow slaves. It is possible that black
workers respected the drivers and looked to them as leaders, for, as Genovese observes,

it is obvious that if the drivers were as they are reported to
have been, they would have had their throats cut as soon
as their white protectors had left. In my own researches for

the war years I have found repeatedly, almost monoto-
nously, that when the slaves fled the plantations or else took
over plantations deserted by the whites, the drivers emerged
as the leaders. Moreover, the runaway records from the
North and from Canada reveal that a number of drivers
were among those who successfully escaped the South.[14]

There were not, as Genovese points out, many slave re-
bellions. Perhaps it is surprising that even a few occurred,
for, considering the enormous power of the whites, rebellion
was suicide. Slavery by definition is stacked heavily against
the slaves. As an institution it is inhumane, but like any
institution, basically it involves human beings. Slaves,
Genovese concludes,

> struggled to live as much as possible on their own terms.
> If their actions were less bombastic and heroic than ro-
> mantic historians would like us to believe, they were none-
> theless impressive in their assertion of their resourcefulness
> and dignity, and a strong sense of self and community. Had
> they not been, the fate of black America after emancipation
> would have been even grimmer than it was. For the most
> part the best that the slaves could do was to live, not merely
> physically but with as much inner autonomy as was humanly
> possible.[15]

The Profitability and Benefits of Slavery

Since antebellum days, men have argued about the profitability of slavery as an economic and human system. Argu-
ments usually focus on the questions: profitable for whom
—the slave, the slaveowner, the South, or the American
economy as a whole? The debate has produced no consensus.

The essence of the economic antislavery argument was
that slavery made and kept the South a backward part of
the nation. Hinton R. Helper, a North Carolinian, summarized this thesis in the 1850's in his *The Impending
Crisis in the South:*

[14] Ibid., p. 42.
[15] Ibid., pp. 42–43.

... The causes which have impeded the progress and prosperity of the South, which have swindled our commerce, and other similar pursuits, into the most contemptible insignificance; sunk a large majority of our people in galling poverty and ignorance, rendered a small minority conceited and tyrannical, and driven the rest away from their homes; entailed upon us a humiliating dependence on the Free States; disgraced us in the recesses of our own souls, and brought us under reproach in the eyes of all civilized and enlightened nations—may all be traced to one common source, and there find solution in the most hateful and horrible word, that was ever incorporated into the vocabulary of human economy—*Slavery!*

Helper believed that since the close of the eighteenth century, the economic development of the South had fallen steadily behind that of the North. He argued that the South lagged behind even in agriculture—and the reason was slavery. Helper listed three reasons why slavery was economically destructive: (1) slaves were kept in ignorance and were thus unable to develop skills or cope with machines; (2) capital was frozen in slave labor and therefore unavailable for investment in other enterprises; and (3) slavery hindered the growth of a home market for local industry.

Cassius Clay, a Kentuckian exiled from the South because of abolitionist propaganda he published in his newspaper, agreed with Helper. Wrote Clay:

The twelve hundred millions of capital invested in slaves is a dead loss to the South; the North getting the same number of laborers doing double the work, for the interest on the money; and sometimes by partnerships, or joint operations, or when men work on their own account, without any interest being expended for labor. ...

Lawyers, merchants, mechanics, laborers, who are your consumers; Robert Wickliffe's two hundred slaves? How many clients do you find, how many goods do you sell, how many hats, coats, saddles, and trunks, do you make for these two hundred slaves? Does Mr. Wickliffe lay out as much for himself and his two hundred slaves, as two hundred freemen do. . . ? Under the free system the towns would grow and furnish a home market to the farmers, which in turn would employ more labor; which would consume the manufactures of the towns, and we could then find our business continually increasing, so that our children might settle down among us and make industrious, honest citizens.[16]

The defenders of slavery as an economically productive system often stressed its benefits to Negroes. They asserted that the system represented social and humanitarian improvement for the African black. William Grayson, in his poem "The Hireling and the Slave," published in 1856, stated the argument:

> Instructed thus, and in the only school
> Barbarians ever know—a master's rule,
> The Negro learns each civilizing art
> That softens and subdues the savage heart,
> Assumes the tone of those with whom he lives,
> Acquires the habit that refinement gives,
> And slowly learns, but surely, while a slave,
> The lessons that his country never gave.
>
> No better mode can human wits discern,
> No happier system wealth or virtue find,
> To tame and elevate the Negro mind.

Furthermore, said Grayson, the only way labor and capital could exist in harmony was through slavery. Because capital and labor were united in the slave, he was better cared for, free of the tensions, uncertainties, and privations of Northern wage earners, and perhaps more free than they in spirit.

> And yet the life, so unassailed by care,
> So blessed with moderate work, with ample fare,
> With all the good the starving pauper needs,
> The happier Slave on each plantation leads,
> Safe from harassing doubts and annual fears,

[16] Quoted in Harold Woodman, "The Profitability of Slavery, a Historical Perennial," *The Journal of Southern History* 29 (1963): 304–305.

He dreads no famine, in unfruitful years;
If harvests fail from inauspicious skies,
The master's providence his food supplies. . . .

The cabin home, not comfortless, though rude,
Light daily labor, and abundant food,
The sturdy health, that temperate habits yield,
The cheerful song, that rings in every field,
The long, loud laugh, that freemen seldom share. . . .

Guarded from want, from beggary secure,
He never feels what hireling crowds endure,
Nor knows, like them, in hapless want to crave,
For wife and child, the comforts of the slave,
Or the sad thought that, when about to die,
He leaves them to the cold world's charity,
And sees them slowly seek the poor-house door—
The last, vile, hated refuge of the poor.

George Fitzhugh in his *Sociology for the South,* published in 1854, said much the same thing in prose as Grayson did in verse. Few free laborers owned their houses, their employment was uncertain, and they had no security and could expect no help when illness struck or when old age came. Competition was the bane of free workers; it blunted and debased them, causing jealousy, rivalries, and hatred among everyone. Negroes had no such problems, and they could depend on masters to care for them in misfortune and ill health and during their old age. Free society never could give such protection. To Fitzhugh, slavery was a positive good.

Proslavery writers concluded that the system strengthened the nation's economy. They emphasized the importance of cotton as the major product of slave labor, asserting that it was a boon to northern textile manufacturers and the largest single cash export the country had. Therefore, they reasoned, slavery was profitable for the nation.

The Abolitionists

Abolitionists nursed no doubts about slavery. They were against the institution—bitterly, unequivocally, and unremittingly.

THE DIS-UNITED STATES—A BLACK BUSINESS.

In this English cartoon, published in 1856, the gentleman represents the South and the farmer represents the North.

The abolitionist crusade began during the first administration of Andrew Jackson with William Lloyd Garrison's declaration of war on slavery, and it ended nearly thirty-five years later when Abraham Lincoln signed the Emancipation Proclamation. Three turbulent decades witnessed a continuing moral assault on southern institutions and, for abolitionists, many encounters with northern resistance that included sharp skirmishes with mobs and great controversies within political parties.

The crusade was characterized by religious fervor, a sense of moral urgency, and a vision of human perfection. At first it was only one of many reform movements that included temperance, the extension of educational opportunity, and the establishment of asylums for the mentally ill. Ultimately, abolitionism became the most important movement of all. It posed difficult questions for contemporaries and it is no less controversial today; historians continue to debate fundamental questions about the origins, significance, and effects of abolitionism in the United States.

The institution of slavery was debated at the Constitutional Convention in 1787. Some members favored its abolition then, but the most that was achieved was a compromise concerning the slave trade. In the 1780's many men fully expected slavery to die out naturally because it was economically unfeasible, but the cotton gin put an end to such hopes.

The idea of abolition did not die, however. The leader of the movement in the 1820's was a mild-mannered Quaker, Benjamin Lundy, who circulated a modest publication entitled *Genius of Universal Emancipation* in which he urged freedom for all men. The impact was slight. The American Colonization Society, founded in 1817, took more direct action, for this group's objective was to move the problem across the ocean. Colonization Society members purchased slaves and set them free to colonize Liberia and Sierra Leone in Africa. After fourteen years, they had given freedom to only 1,420 slaves. During this time, approximately 100,000 Negro babies were born into slavery in the United States. The colonization idea proved impractical. Between 1820 and 1860 the number of slaves in the United States quadrupled, and the value of the average slave rose from $400 to $1,000 and even to $1,500. With each passing year slavery rooted itself more deeply in American society. The American Colonization Society could not begin to raise the amount of money needed to halt the rapidly growing slave system.

William Lloyd Garrison.

In 1831 opposition to slavery entered a new and more vigorous phase. On January 1, the first issue of a new paper called the *Liberator* appeared in Boston, edited by William Lloyd Garrison, who in his first editorial proclaimed:

I will be as harsh as truth, and as uncompromising as justice. On this subject [slavery] I do not wish to think, to speak, or write, with moderation. No! No! Tell a man whose house is on fire to give a moderate alarm; tell him to moderately rescue his wife from the hands of the ravisher; tell the mother to gradually extricate her babe from the fire into which it has fallen; but urge me not to use moderation in

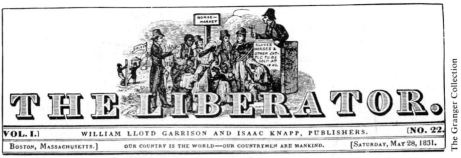

The Granger Collection

The masthead of William Lloyd Garrison's abolitionist journal, *The Liberator*, proclaimed, "Our Country Is the World—Our Countrymen Are Mankind."

a cause like the present! I am in earnest—I will not equivocate—I will not excuse—I will not retreat a single inch—AND I WILL BE HEARD.

As abolitionism gained momentum, well-known lecturers and writers joined the crusade. Lucretia Mott, Theodore Parker, John Greenleaf Whittier, James Russell Lowell, Wendell Phillips, and Ralph Waldo Emerson gave their time and talent to lecturing and writing for the antislavery cause. In 1833 the movement gained additional strength from the American Anti-Slavery Society formed in that year. At its height, some 2,000 local antislavery societies claimed a combined membership of about 200,000.

In many parts of the country during the 1830's and 1840's, the increased militancy of abolitionists and the abolitionist movement aroused bitter opposition. Northern wage earners, fearing job competition from free Negroes, often broke up antislavery meetings. Northern businessmen believed that the movement impaired their trade with the South. Abolitionist leaders were subject to abuse, and they were often attacked, barred from clubs, and jailed. One abolitionist editor, Elijah Lovejoy of Alton, Illinois, was murdered by an angry mob. William Lloyd Garrison himself once was dragged through the streets by an inflamed crowd of antiabolitionists.

Abolitionists used a number of methods to arouse public opinion. They lectured, wrote, submitted petitions to state legislatures, and organized underground railroads—the

LIBERTY LINE.
NEW ARRANGEMENT---NIGHT AND DAY.

The improved and splendid Locomotives, Clarkson and Lundy, with their trains fitted up in the best style of accommodation for passengers, will run their regular trips during the present season, between the borders of the Patriarchal Dominion and Libertyville, Upper Canada. Gentlemen and Ladies, who may wish to improve their health or circumstances, by a northern tour; are respectfully invited to give us their patronage.

SEATS FREE, *irrespective of color.*

Necessary Clothing furnished gratuitously to such as have "*fallen among thieves.*"

"Hide the outcasts—let the oppressed go free."—*Bible.*

☞For seats apply at any of the trap doors, or to the conductor of the train.

J. CROSS, *Proprietor.*

N. B. For the special benefit of Pro-Slavery Police Officers, an extra heavy wagon for Texas, will be furnished, whenever it may be necessary, in which they will be forwarded as dead freight, to the "Valley of Rascals," always at the risk of the owners.

☞Extra Overcoats provided for such of them as are afflicted with protracted *chilly-phobia.*

This "advertisement" for the underground railroad appeared in the *Western Citizen* on July 13, 1844.

name given the practice of moving slaves from point to point at night and hiding them by day until they reached a land of freedom, often Canada. Even so, the abolitionists never managed to wield much political strength or make enough of an impression on northern public opinion to swing it firmly against slavery. The Liberty party selected James G. Birney as a candidate for president in 1840 and he polled only 7,000 votes. In the next presidential election the Liberty party did a little better, but still its candidate drew only 62,300 of the 2,500,000 votes cast. In 1848 the Free Soil party, interested mainly in keeping slavery out of new territories, ran former president Martin Van Buren. The Free Soil group proved stronger than the Liberty party candidates, but Van Buren failed to win enough votes to defeat his Whig and Democratic opponents.

Some abolitionists had temporary success when they attacked slavery in state courts. One such case occurred in Wisconsin in the 1850's. Joshua Glover, a runaway slave from Missouri, had enjoyed two years of freedom in Racine, Wisconsin, before he was betrayed and recaptured on the night of March 10, 1854. Glover's card game with some friends was interrupted by five men, led by his former master Benjamin S. Garland, who burst in and seized and handcuffed him. Glover did not submit peacefully, but it was an uneven struggle. A few minutes later, his head battered and bleeding, he was lying bound in a wagon on his way to Milwaukee and jail, first stop on his return to bondage in Missouri.

Wisconsin in the 1850's, however, was not an area sympathetic to slavery or slave-catching. Former New Englanders in the state, as well as German and Norwegian immigrants, strongly opposed slavery. Wisconsin also had Sherman M. Booth, a fiery abolitionist editor. Born in New England, Booth began his newspaper career with the *American Freeman*, an antislavery publication, in the town of Waukesha. The more conservative *Milwaukee Sentinel* dismissed Booth's paper in 1845 as a "miserable driveling concern that is all the while whining and sniveling at the community for its lack of patronage. This sheet, which on every one of its irregular and abortive appearances froths and foams with long-drawn slush pails of stale abolition twaddle . . . is a political curiosity." This was not an untypical expression of many people's attitude toward abolitionism.

In 1852 Booth moved his presses to Milwaukee and renamed his paper the *Daily Free Democrat*. There he continued to preach abolitionism and write extensively about Free Soil, which he supported, and the Fugitive Slave Law of 1850, which he opposed.

Booth heard about Glover's capture soon after it occurred. He and some friends converged on the Milwaukee jail as soon as Glover was lodged there, battered down the door, removed him, and took him back to Racine. There they put him on a boat bound for Canada.

The following Monday morning Booth's newspaper proclaimed "greetings to the Free States of the Union, that, in Wisconsin, the Fugitive Slave Law is repealed! The first attempt to enforce the law, in this state, has signally, gloriously failed."

STOCKHOLDERS
OF THE UNDERGROUND
R. R. COMPANY
Hold on to Your Stock!!

This Detroit newspaper article, dated April 19, 1853, announces the arrival of twenty-nine escaped slaves, who are en route to freedom in Canada. The article solicits money, farm tools, and clothes to help the slaves start their new lives.

Federal officials took a different view of the matter. A marshal arrested Booth and charged him with aiding Glover's escape, an action contrary to the Fugitive Slave Law. A United States commissioner found him guilty and ordered him held for trial, freeing Booth in the meantime on $2,000 bond. Booth's lawyer, Byron Paine, appealed to the Wisconsin Supreme Court to block federal action, and during the hearing Paine argued that the fugitive slave clause of the Constitution, in Article IV, represented a mere compact between the states. He contended that if a state did not wish to be bound by it and return fugitive slaves, neither a slaveholding state nor the federal government could force it to. Moreover, he asked the court to declare the Fugitive Slave Law of 1850 unconstitutional, which it did. The Wisconsin court thus adopted the same position with respect to states' rights that South Carolina had in 1832.

Sherman M. Booth did not get off, however. He was later re-arrested by federal officers, tried, and convicted, and a federal court in Milwaukee sentenced him to one month in jail and fined him $1,000.

Once again, Booth and Paine appealed to the Wisconsin Supreme Court, and once again the court declared the Fugitive Slave Law unconstitutional. It also said that a state had the power to free anyone illegally imprisoned. At the time, Wisconsin public opinion generally seemed to be behind the court.

The United States Supreme Court had the final word. The Booth case finally reached the Court on appeal in December, 1858, and the justices made short work of the Wisconsin decision. No state-issued writ had any authority in a federal case, the Court said, and the Fugitive Slave Law was indeed constitutional. Moreover, no state court could interfere with the judgment and proceedings of a federal court. The Court ordered Booth returned to the custody of federal officers.

The state of Wisconsin refused. Consequently, a United States marshal once again arrested Booth and placed him in the Milwaukee jail. Friends quietly entered the jail, removed Booth from his cell, and placed the jailer there instead. Then they hurried the abolitionist out of town.

"Liberty, the Fair Maid of Kansas in the Hands of Border Ruffians," a cartoon reflecting the Republican reaction to the Kansas-Nebraska Act of 1854.

Booth spent the next several months on an underground railroad of his own, popping up here and there to speak to abolitionist groups in eastern Wisconsin. In the fall, however, he was recaptured and returned to jail, where he stayed until the spring of 1859. As one of his last acts in office, President James Buchanan pardoned Booth and remitted his fine.

The Booth case and other incidents of abolitionist success served only to arouse public opinion in the South. And in Congress, thanks in part to the abolitionist crusade, positions and attitudes polarized after the passage of the Kansas-Nebraska Act in 1854.

Far from settling the slavery issue, the passage of the Kansas-Nebraska Act, which left it up to those territories to decide for or against slavery, simply made Kansas a battleground. Southerners moved quickly into Kansas, determined to secure it for slavery, and there were met by equally adamant antislavery northerners armed with rifles shipped in boxes labeled "Bibles" from New England. The territory quickly became known as "bleeding Kansas."

In the Senate on May 19, 1856, Charles Sumner of

SOUTHERN CHIVALRY — ARGUMENT versus CLUB'S.

On May 22, 1856, Congressman Preston S. Brooks expressed his disapproval of Senator Charles Sumner's views on Kansas by beating Sumner unconscious.

Massachusetts arose to speak on "The Crime Against Kansas." A confirmed and militant abolitionist, Sumner was also a master of sarcasm and invective. The behavior of proslavery partisans in Kansas, he said, constituted "the rape of a virgin territory." Southerners in that land were "murderous robbers." Using even more insulting language as he warmed to his subject, Sumner flayed southerners for their position on slavery and Kansas, and singled out in particular the senator from South Carolina, Andrew Butler.

Southerners did not receive Sumner's attack meekly, nor was their language gentle when they responded. Clement C. Clay of Alabama called Sumner "a sneaking, sinuous, snake-like poltroon." Another southern senator declared that he deserved nothing less than hanging from the nearest tree. Even some northern senators were appalled. Stephen A. Douglas of Illinois labeled the speech "obscene," and went on to say, "It is his object to provoke some one of us to kick him as one would a dog in the street, that he may get sympathy from the just chastisement." Douglas's re-

Charles Sumner of Massachusetts.

action, of course, could have been expected since he had been the principal architect of the Kansas-Nebraska plan of popular sovereignty.

Two days after the speech, working at his desk in the Senate, Sumner glanced up to find Preston S. Brooks, representative from South Carolina, standing over him. "I have read your speech twice over," Brooks said to Sumner. "It's a libel on South Carolina and on Mr. Butler, who is a friend of mine," and, as Brooks might have added but did not, a kinsman. With that, before Sumner could reply or stand, Brooks began to smash him over the head with his cane. He laid on blow after blow, finally breaking the cane, but continuing to beat Sumner with the shattered remnant until the senator collapsed unconscious on the floor.

Now it was the turn of northern people to be indignant. Abolitionist Horace Greeley, editor of the *New York Tribune,* considered Brooks' act a normal expression of southern character by an "almost sainted champion of slaveholding dominance" who would not hesitate "at an assault or a murder." This was a fair example of northern opinion in general, and there were many demands for Brooks' punishment.

Many southerners regretted the incident because it played into abolitionist hands, yet few called it unjustified. Southerners in Congress rallied to Brooks' defense and their votes prevented him from being expelled. He then resigned, but his constituents re-elected him with only six votes cast against him. They, like most southerners, believed that Sumner had got what he deserved, and newspaper editors published a great deal of invective against the Massachusetts senator along with high praise for Brooks and the southern point of view. Many residents of the South sent replacement canes to Brooks, one of which was inscribed "Hit Him Again." Brooks was later arrested and tried for assault, but a sympathetic judge of southern extraction in Washington, D.C., merely fined him $300. Charles Sumner remained out of the Senate for three years, and the people of Massachusetts left his seat vacant while he recuperated. By the time he returned, in 1859, feelings had become so intense that some members of Congress were wearing sidearms to the sessions.

The traditional interpretation of abolitionism viewed it as a religious crusade centered in New England under the leadership of William Lloyd Garrison. Because they believed that slavery was contrary to the laws of nature, the abolitionists felt justified in destroying it. To them, human bondage was intolerable in a democratic society, and all nineteenth-century histories described Garrison as a man of heroic stature.

In 1933, Gilbert Barnes published *The Antislavery Impulse,* an important work on the abolitionists. Barnes agreed that abolitionism was a religious crusade, but he argued that it was not centered in New England and that Garrison was not its leader. He suggested that the movement originated in western Pennsylvania, western New York, and Ohio. Furthermore, Barnes contended that Garrison was not even a typical abolitionist, let alone the movement's leader. He described Garrison, because of his fervor, as a liability to the national movement. Among the real leaders, according to Barnes, were Theodore Weld, a prominent abolitionist writer and lecturer; James G. Birney, a southern planter who freed his slaves and went north to work for the abolitionist cause, becoming executive secretary of the Anti-Slavery Society in 1837 and the Liberty party's presidential candidate in 1840; and Arthur and Lewis Tappan, brothers and partners in a prosperous silk business in Massachusetts. The Tappans were at first active in the Anti-Slavery Society with Garrison but withdrew in 1840 to organize their own abolitionist group, the American and Foreign Anti-Slavery Society. A third Tappan brother, Benjamin, represented Ohio in the United States Senate from 1839 to 1845, where he championed the abolitionist cause.

Russel Nye and John Thomas have attempted to combine the elements of western abolitionism with those of the New England group, stressing the importance of both parts of the movement. Thomas, for example, has argued that the

Abolitionist John Brown on his way to the gallows.

western branch of abolitionism was planned and organized by transplanted New Englanders and was thus a product and extension of New England culture.

In addition to debating its origins and leadership, historians have also disagreed on abolitionism's effects and on the merits of the behavior of abolitionists. Avery Craven, for example, considered the abolitionists irresponsible fanatics and laid on them much of the blame for the outbreak of war in 1861. According to him, they created an atmosphere of fear, hatred, and hysteria that prevented the use of reason. The result was civil war. C. Vann Woodward has stated that John Brown's raid on Harper's Ferry, Virginia, in 1859, during which he sought to capture a federal arsenal as a part of his plan to free the slaves forcibly, was crucial to the thinking and behavior of abolitionists. It was, in Woodward's view, a "crisis of means," and thereafter the abolitionists idealized Brown and compromised their original creed of nonviolence. Militant tactics became fully acceptable in the struggle to destroy slavery.

The student of abolitionism is left with many significant questions. Do ends justify means in a righteous cause? Were the abolitionists farsighted realists who awakened the American people to the evils of slavery? Or were they irresponsible fanatics, spawning fear, hatred, hysteria, and ultimately civil war in the reckless pursuit of their goal?

John Brown.

SUGGESTED READINGS

Barnes, Gilbert. *The Antislavery Impulse: 1830–1844.* Harcourt Brace Jovanovich, Harbinger Books.

Bennett, Lerone, Jr. *Before the Mayflower: A History of the Negro in America, 1619–1964.* Penguin, Pelican Books.

Botkin, Benjamin A., ed. *Lay My Burden Down: A Folk History of Slavery.* University of Chicago Press, Phoenix Books.

Elkins, Stanley M. *Slavery: A Problem in American Institutional and Intelleceual Life.* University of Chicago Press.

Franklin, John Hope. *From Slavery to Freedom: A History of Negro Americans.* Random House, Vintage Books.

Genovese, Eugene D. *The Political Economy of Slavery: Studies in the Economy and Society of the Slave South.* Random House, Vintage Books.

McKitrick, Eric L., ed. *Slavery Defended: The Views of the Old South.* Prentice-Hall, Spectrum Books.

Rozwenc, Edwin. *Slavery as a Cause of the Civil War.* D. C. Heath.

Stampp, Kenneth. *The Peculiar Institution.* Random House, Vintage Books.

Thomas, John L., ed. *Slavery Attacked: The Abolitionist Crusade.* Prentice-Hall, Spectrum Books.

Wish, Harvey. *Slavery in the South.* Farrar, Straus & Giroux, Noonday Press.

Lincoln's Inauguration, March 4, 1865. Directly below Lincoln are three of the men who would conspire with J.W. Booth to kill Lincoln and other members of the government. The tall man in the gray hat is Lewis Paine, and the men on his right and left are co-conspirators. Booth himself is on the platform directly above Lincoln, but is not visible in this picture.

CHAPTER FOUR

ABRAHAM LINCOLN

A crucial question about the movement toward civil conflict concerns the quality of statesmanship in both the North and the South. Many scholars have concluded that the generation of the 1850's and 1860's was, except for Lincoln, devoid of statesmanship. President James Buchanan, for example, has been found sadly lacking in leadership qualities, and congressmen of that era have been described as even less endowed than the president. Both houses of Congress overflowed with contentious men alert to any slight to their section of the country, looking at every legislative proposal solely from a sectional point of view.

In his *Statesmanship of the Civil War*, Allan Nevins discussed criteria by which to judge great leaders, measured against which all save one of the Civil War generation fell far short.

> . . . We require intellectual power; we require moral strength —weight of character; and we require something more— an instinct for the spirit and needs of a critical time. In eras of good feeling and quiet, and in placid, provincial societies, no statesmen appear; and every crisis demands its special leadership, of a type and quality for which the past seldom affords precedent. . . .
>
> To divine the hopes, fears, moods, appetites, and opinions of a democracy in time of crisis, a leader needs an instinctive understanding of the masses—a sort of sixth sense which seldom comes without long experience; and to mold public sentiment the greatest leaders need not only ability and character, but some kind of passion. . . .

> Without passion, a leader may meet the problems of
> his day with sober practical wisdom. . . . But he can never
> meet them with inspiration, the inspiration that is the chief
> hallmark of a truly great statesman. . . .[1]

Nevins surveyed the careers of the leaders of the Confederacy—Jefferson Davis, Alexander Stephens, Judah P. Benjamin, Christopher Memminger, John Breckenridge, Stephen Mallory, John Reagan—and concluded that they all lacked the necessary qualities. And among the leaders of the Union—Abraham Lincoln, Hannibal Hamlin, William Seward, Salmon P. Chase, Edwin Stanton, Edward Bates, Montgomery Blair, Gideon Wells, Caleb Smith—Nevins listed only Lincoln among history's great statesmen. What made Lincoln great?

Speaking before a joint session of Congress on the 150th anniversary of Lincoln's birth, Carl Sandburg said, "Not often in the pages of history does there appear a man who is both hard as steel and soft as the drifting fog."[2] As these words indicate, it has long been the fashion for writers to view Lincoln romantically, not realistically. When a man has become so famous that his name is known to everyone, his identity is likely to be lost. All the subtleties and inconsistencies that make up the real man are forgotten or suppressed. Finally he becomes as lifeless as his statue.

No one in American history has suffered more from this process than Abraham Lincoln. Long familiarity with his name and his appearance has made us feel that we know all about this man. We remember all the little things about his dress—the unpressed, ill-fitting clothes, the high silk hat, and the little black tie, always askew. His honesty, his kindness, and his passion for justice are familiar to Americans from their childhood days.

The Lincoln so firmly fixed in our minds is not a person but a concept. The man himself was much deeper and more vital. His character was extraordinarily complex. His motives are not easily understood, and they have often been

[1] Allan Nevins, *The Statesmanship of the Civil War* (New York: Macmillan Co., 1962), pp. 5, 8–9. Copyright © 1953, 1962 by Macmillan Publishing Co., Inc.

[2] *Congressional Record*, 12 February 1959, p. 1.

Library of Congress

Library of Congress

These photographs of Lincoln were taken in June, 1860, at Springfield, Illinois.

misinterpreted. Contrary to popular belief, his rise to fame was neither accidental nor unsought. And, more important than anything else, Lincoln was a human being, with human weaknesses, faults, and frailties. It is a confirmation of his greatness that despite his flaws he still seems great, and that he grows even more interesting on closer study.

It is often forgotten that Lincoln's accomplishments as a politician made possible his accomplishments as a statesman. His primary obligation was to get elected to office. If he had not been elected president in 1860, Lincoln would appear in history as only a minor politician from Illinois. Had he been defeated for re-election in 1864, he probably would have been written off as a failure, a man who presided without effect over a country destroying itself through civil war. It is important, therefore, to understand that Abraham Lincoln was a master at the art of politics.

That Lincoln should have won election at all and then achieve extraordinary stature in history is astonishing in light of his low standing among many of his contemporaries.

He did not have the support of the press, the politicians, or even the majority of the people. The newspapers abused him as "a slang-whanging stump speaker," "half-witted," "mole-eyed monster," a poor punster, a baboon, a simpleton, the original gorilla, a smutty joker, and a first-rate *second-rate* man. Critics openly called him a "political coward," "timid and ignorant," and a man of "no education." The *New York Herald*, among the most powerful newspapers of the day, declared:

> President Lincoln is a joke incarnated. His election was a
> very sorry joke. The idea that such a man as he should be
> President of such a country as this is a very ridiculous
> joke. . . . His inaugural address was a joke, since it was full
> of promises which he has never performed. His Cabinet
> is and always has been a standing joke. All his State papers
> are jokes. . . . His intrigues to secure a renomination and
> the hopes he appears to entertain of a re-election are,
> however, the most laughable jokes of all.[3]

The fact that in 1861 Lincoln was a minority president demonstrated the slimness of his public support. In the off-year elections of 1862 the Lincoln administration lost control of New York, Pennsylvania, Ohio, Indiana, and Illinois. Although Lincoln failed to win much support from the press, the politicians, and the people, he nevertheless kept his party and himself in power by winning in 1864, being the first president since Andrew Jackson to be re-elected. His astute and relentless operation of a political machine enabled him to do this.

Much has been written about the extraordinary political skills revealed in Lincoln the president, but anyone who examines his career during the preceding decade will find ample evidence of this same quality. Historian David Donald described Lincoln as the master wire-puller of the state Republican organization in Illinois.

Behind that facade of humble directness and folksy humor,

---

[3] Quoted in David Donald, *Lincoln Reconsidered: Essays on the Civil War* (New York: Random House, Vintage Books, 1956), p. 74.

Lincoln was moving steadily toward his object; by 1860 he had maneuvered himself into a position where he controlled the party machinery, platform, and candidates of one of the pivotal states in the Union. A Chicago lawyer who had known Lincoln intimately for three decades summarized these pre-presidential years: "One great public mistake . . . generally received and acquiesced in, is that he is considered by the people of this country as a frank, guileless, and unsophisticated man. There never was a greater mistake. . . . He handled and moved men remotely as we do pieces upon a chessboard."[4]

Don Fehrenbacher in his *Prelude to Greatness* also commented on Lincoln's skills in Illinois politics, saying that

> . . . if greatness is the response of inner strength to an extraordinary challenge, Lincoln had first met such a challenge and begun to show such strength in 1854, after the repeal of the Missouri Compromise. Never in the presidency did he surpass the political skill with which he shaped the Republican party of Illinois, held it together, and made himself its leader. In his relations with other Illinoisans one finds the same patience and respect for human dignity that characterized the wartime president. Ambition drove him hard in these years of preparation, and yet it was an ambition notably free of pettiness, malice, and overindulgence. It was, moreover, an ambition leavened by moral conviction and a deep faith in the principles upon which the republic had been built. The Lincoln of the 1860's was much the same man under greater challenge.[5]

Lincoln brought to the executive office a clear understanding of the traits of the successful politician. For example, whenever possible he avoided discussing his ideas and policies, refusing to commit himself in advance to any course of action. Even men considered to be his close associates did not enjoy Lincoln's complete confidence. He was

[4] Ibid., pp. 66–67.

[5] Don Fehrenbacher, *Prelude to Greatness: Lincoln in the 1850's* (Palo Alto, Calif.: Stanford University Press, 1962), p. 161. Reprinted with permission of the publisher.

The bombardment of Fort Sumter from Fort Moultrie, April 12 and 13, 1861.

described as a profound mystery, reticent, silent, and a
sphinx. His most frequent reply to questions concerning
policy was, "My policy is to have no policy." On other
occasions he would reply with a long and humorous story
totally unrelated to an important question to which someone demanded an answer. David Donald has pointed out
that Lincoln could say much in few words when he chose,
but he could also say nothing at great length when he found
it expedient.

Crisis at Fort Sumter

Few incidents in the war so strikingly reflect Lincoln's political astuteness as his management of the crisis at Fort
Sumter. One view of his behavior and the reasons behind
it has been presented by Charles W. Ramsdell. Much of the
following discussion rests on his research.[6]

The Confederate leaders who ordered the bombardment
of Fort Sumter were neither incompetent nor irresponsible.
They were fully aware of the danger of initiating hostilities
and, according to Ramsdell, they did all they could to

[6] Charles W. Ramsdell, "Lincoln and Fort Sumter," *The Journal
of Southern History* 3 (1937): 259–288.

CHARLESTON

MERCURY

EXTRA:

Passed unanimously at 1.15 o'clock, P. M. December 20th, 1860.

AN ORDINANCE

To dissolve the Union between the State of South Carolina and other States united with her under the compact entitled " The Constitution of the United States of America."

We, the People of the State of South Carolina, in Convention assembled, do declare and ordain, and it is hereby declared and ordained,

That the Ordinance adopted by us in Convention, on the twenty-third day of May, in the year of our Lord one thousand seven hundred and eighty-eight, whereby the Constitution of the United States of America was ratified, and also, all Acts and parts of Acts of the General Assembly of this State, ratifying amendments of the said Constitution, are hereby repealed; and that the union now subsisting between South Carolina and other States, under the name of "The United States of America," is hereby dissolved.

THE

UNION

IS

DISSOLVED!

avoid it. Why was it, then, that they finally assumed the role of aggressor?

On December 20, 1860, the state legislature of South Carolina, by unanimous vote, declared that "the Union now subsisting between South Carolina and the other states, under the name of the 'United States of America,' is hereby dissolved." South Carolina's secession came hard upon the announcement of Lincoln's election as president. Lincoln had received less than forty percent of the popular vote, nationwide, but he had carried every northern state. He was clearly a northern president; southern leaders believed that he was also an abolitionist president, that under him "the slaveholding states will no longer have the power of self-government."

By February 1, 1861, six more southern states had seceded—Georgia, Mississippi, Florida, Alabama, Louisiana, and Texas. On February 4, delegates from six of the seceded states met in Montgomery, Alabama, to frame a new government, the Confederate States of America. The convention drafted a constitution modeled upon the United States Constitution but emphasizing states' rights and guaranteeing slavery in all the states, and elected Jefferson Davis of Mississippi and Alexander Stephens of Georgia as provisional president and vice-president. The convention also appointed commissioners to negotiate with the government of the United States. The commissioners were to look into the matter of taking over federal property in the southern states—post offices, customs houses, and military bases. In fact, the seceded states had already seized the federal forts and arsenals within their borders, with two exceptions— Fort Pickens, near Pensacola, Florida, and Fort Sumter, in Charleston, South Carolina.

The Fort Sumter question first arose in January, 1860, when a relief ship ordered to the fort by President Buchanan was turned back. Only the intervention of other southern leaders restrained South Carolina officials from ordering an attack on the fort then. In February, the leaders of the newly organized Confederate government removed the responsibility of making a decision concerning Fort Sumter from the hands of Governor Francis Pickens of South Carolina

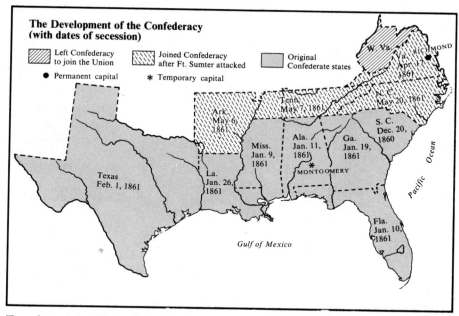

The Development of the Confederacy
(with dates of secession)

Left Confederacy to join the Union | Joined Confederacy after Ft. Sumter attacked | Original Confederate states

● Permanent capital   * Temporary capital

W. Va.   Va. RICHMOND ● Apr. 17, 1861

Tenn. May 7, 1861   N.C. May 20, 1861

Ark. May 6, 1861   S.C. Dec. 20, 1860

Miss. Jan. 9, 1861   Ala. Jan. 11, 1861   Ga. Jan. 19, 1861

Texas Feb. 1, 1861   La. Jan. 26, 1861   *MONTGOMERY

Pacific Ocean

Fla. Jan. 10, 1861

Gulf of Mexico

Two slave states, Kentucky and Missouri, did not secede, and the loyalist counties of western Virginia joined the Union as a separate state in 1863.

because they feared his impatience and thought he might precipitate a war at any time. They did not want the South to appear as the aggressor.

The problem concerning Fort Sumter was clear. If the Union withdrew its forces, it would be acknowledging the legality of secession. Southern leaders, on the other hand, considered the Confederacy an independent government. They could not permit another government to hold a fort that threatened a principal city. The situation remained a stalemate until Lincoln assumed the presidency on March 4, 1861. Both sides anxiously awaited a statement of policy. Lincoln made it clear in his inaugural address that he regarded the Union as unbroken, and that he would enforce federal laws in all states without the use of violence whenever possible. Lincoln further stated,

> The power confided in me will be used to hold, occupy and possess the property and places belonging to the gov-

dissatisfied, hold the right side in the dispute, there still is no single good reason for precipitate action. Intelligence, patriotism, Christianity, and a firm reliance on Him, who has never yet forsaken this favored land, are still competent to adjust, in the best way, all our present difficulty.

In *your* hands, my dissatisfied fellow countrymen, and not in *mine*, is the momentous issue of civil war. The government will not assail *you*. You can have no conflict, without being yourselves the aggressors. You have no oath registered in Heaven to destroy the government, while *I* shall have the most solemn one to "preserve, protect and defend" it.

I am loth to close. We are not enemies, but friends— We must not be enemies. Though passion may have strained, it must not break our bonds of affection. The mystic chords of memory, streching from every battle field, and patriot grave, to every living heart and hearth stone, all over this broad land, will yet swell the chorus of the Union, when again touched, as surely they will be by the better angels of our nature.

The closing words of Lincoln's first inaugural address, delivered March 4, 1861.

ernment, and to collect the duties and imposts; but beyond what may be necessary for these objects, there will be no invasion, no using of force against or among the people everywhere. . . . In your hands, my dissatisfied fellow countrymen, and not in mine, is the momentous issue of civil war. The government will not assail you. You can have no conflict without being yourselves the aggressors.

He avoided committing himself to any course of action because caution was both expedient and wise. Professor Ramsdell has asserted that Lincoln possessed the extraordinary skill of phrasing his public addresses in such a way as to arouse exactly the reaction he wanted from each special group. The aggressive and militant Republicans interpreted his address as a firm determination to enforce obedience. Northern moderates, peace advocates, and leaders in border states found in the address a conciliatory attitude, while the people of the South thought the address threatening and subsequently hastened their preparations for defense.

Major Robert Anderson, commander at Fort Sumter, sent word to Lincoln on inauguration day that he doubted the stability of his position. On March 15, Lincoln asked his cabinet members for their written opinions on the question of Fort Sumter. Only Postmaster General Montgomery

Blair favored sending a relief expedition. The remainder advised evacuation of Fort Sumter and reinforcement of Fort Pickens.

Public opinion in the North was also divided. The thought of giving up the fort disgusted some people, and they encouraged the president to exert his full authority, even to the extent of declaring war. Peace advocates led the other element of northern public opinion. They feared war and urged a settlement without resorting to arms. If Lincoln followed a strong policy and reinforced Sumter, he would alienate the peace advocates and the people of the border states. If he chose to evacuate the fort, he would be admitting the legality of the Confederacy. If the matter was allowed to drift, Anderson would run out of supplies and be forced to evacuate. Lincoln would then lose the support of the aggressive wing of the Republican party. In any case, the party would be split. Furthermore, the chance of a military victory was almost nonexistent. All avenues of action seemed closed.

At that point, Charles Ramsdell has suggested, Lincoln hit on the idea of inducing the Confederacy to attack Sumter before Anderson ran out of supplies, thus forcing the South into the position of aggressor. Such an event, if managed properly, would unite the two wings of the Republican party, bring in some support from the Democrats, heal the breach in northern public opinion, and perhaps even hold the border states. Who among northerners would object to sending a shipload of food to hungry soldiers? Having had a report from a personal envoy to Governor Pickens, Lincoln knew that any sort of relief to Sumter would result in a southern attack.

Meeting with his cabinet on March 29, Lincoln discovered a marked change in attitude. Only Secretary of State William H. Seward and Secretary of the Interior Caleb Smith favored evacuation of Sumter now. The other members of the cabinet urged reinforcement. On that day Lincoln ordered an expedition to be prepared and ready to move by April 6. In strict secrecy, provision was also made for an expedition to Fort Pickens—an expedition of which only Seward and Lincoln were aware.

Jefferson Davis, president of the Confederacy.

During the afternoon of April 4, Lincoln ordered final preparation for the Sumter expedition. He also wrote a letter to Major Anderson informing him that supplies were coming. On April 6, Lincoln sent the following letter by courier to Governor Pickens of South Carolina over the signature of Simon Cameron, secretary of war:

> I am directed by the President of the United States to notify you to expect an attempt will be made to supply Fort Sumter with provisions only; and that, if such an attempt be not resisted, no effort to throw in men, arms, or ammunition will be made without further notice, or in case of an attack upon the fort.

Lincoln had insisted on writing the letter himself. It was both skillfully phrased and precisely timed. He made the same sentences say different things to different people. Northerners saw no threat in the letter. The government did not propose to use force if it could be avoided. But to Confederate leaders, it not only said that provisions were coming, but it also carried the threat of force if they were not allowed to be brought in. The South interpreted the note as a direct challenge.

Although the Confederates knew that a large expedition was in readiness, they did not know that a portion of it was going to Fort Pickens in Florida. They were permitted to believe that the whole force was coming to Charleston. The letter from President Lincoln was read to Governor Pickens on the evening of April 8. On that same day in Washington, three Confederate representatives were refused a conference with Secretary of State Seward. President Davis was informed of both incidents on April 9. He immediately ordered the confiscation of all mail coming out of Fort Sumter, whereupon Major Anderson's reply to his notification of reinforcement was intercepted and sent immediately to President Davis. Lincoln's timing and planning had been perfect.

Having lost tactical advantage, the South now faced a serious dilemma. The Confederates had either to take the fort before provisions arrived, thereby firing the first shot, or stand by quietly while it was reinforced. Lincoln's strategy had paid off. He was the master either way the Confederacy chose to move. The Southern decision—reluctantly arrived at—was to attack.

The Ramsdell thesis, suggesting that Lincoln maneuvered the Confederacy into the role of aggressor, has been challenged by another Civil War scholar, Richard N. Current:

In this Ramsdell thesis there undoubtedly is a certain element of truth, but there is even more that is fallacious. Ramsdell—like [Jefferson] Davis, [Alexander] Stephens, and others before him—makes Lincoln appear too much the warmonger, the Confederates too much the unoffending devotees of peace. Ramsdell also pictures Lincoln as too much the controlling force, the Confederates as too much the helpless, passive agents.

After all, the Confederates themselves had something to do with the firing on Fort Sumter.

Even assuming that Lincoln had some kind of "maneuver" in mind, he could not have made it work without the co-operation of the Confederates. And it is fair enough to suppose that the maneuver idea in some form did occur to him, since he received so much advice about decoying the enemy into shooting first, and since he was familiar with the idea as applied by President Polk [prior to the Mexican War]. But the point is that Lincoln could have had no sure foreknowledge that an expedition, no matter how well planned and carried out, would have the desired effect. It might have exactly the opposite effect, and indeed he received counter advice telling him so. . . .

If the Confederates had withheld their fire upon the fort, if they had waited for the arrival of the ships and had merely tried to head them off, and if the fort then had opened fire on the installations in the harbor, the Confederates might have had a rallying cry indeed, a cry that would have won them many friends in the North as well as the border states. . . .

There were still other dangers—for Lincoln. If for any reason his expedition was bungled, and the Confederates waited and withheld their fire, then Lincoln and the Union would suffer a psychological blow. And the expedition was in fact bungled, but of course the Confederates did not withhold their fire.

When they did fire, they did not necessarily become the aggressors because of that. To this extent Stephens was correct. By the same token, however, Lincoln did not necessarily bcome the aggressor when he sent the expedition.

From the Confederate point of view the United States had made itself the aggressor long before Lincoln acted to reinforce any fort. It was aggression when, on December 26, 1860, Major Anderson moved his troops from Moultrie to the more defensible Sumter. Indeed, it was a continuing act of aggression every day that Union forces remained in Sumter or any other place within the bounds of the Confederacy. And from the Union point of view the Confederacy had committed and was committing aggression by its very claim to existence, to say nothing of its seizures of Federal property, its occupation of Fort Moultrie, and its construction of a semicircle of harbor batteries with Sumter as their target.

There is little reason to suppose, and there was little reason for Lincoln to suppose, that he could escape either war or the charge of warmonger by giving up Sumter and

The evacuation of Fort Moultrie by U.S. troops, Christmas night, 1860.

holding [Fort] Pickens as a substitute symbol of the national authority. The Confederate commissioners in Washington had instructions to obtain the cession of Pickens and other places as well as Sumter. Lincoln's fact-finding emissary to Charleston, Hurlbut, reported back that conflict could not be averted by Sumter's abandonment. "Undoubtedly this will be followed by a demand for Pickens and the Keys of the Gulf," Hurlbut opined. Indeed, Seward himself at the last did not really believe that Pickens, in contrast to Sumter, could be held and reinforced without war. He merely thought a better case for war could be made in consequence of an incident at Pickens. . . .

No matter which way he turned, Lincoln could find no clear and unobstructed path away from the danger of war. As Hurlbut told him, and as various signs indicated, the sacrifice of Sumter would mean no guarantee of continued peace. "Nor do I believe," Hurlbut added, "that any policy which may be adopted by the Government will prevent the possibility of armed collision."

Of course, a surrender to the Confederate demands might have prevented, or at least postponed, the shooting. When the Confederates talked of peace, that is what they meant— a surrender on Lincoln's part. They wanted peace with the recognition of the Confederacy and the transfer to it of all the property the United States claimed within Confederate boundaries. No doubt Lincoln longed for peace. But peace to him was meaningless without the preservation of the Union.

And even if he had been willing to yield all that the seceders for the moment demanded, he had no assurance that the result would be anything more than a postponement of war, a prolongation of the truce. One possibility is this: the rest of the slave states might have remained in the Union, and the seven states of the stunted Confederacy might have had eventually no good choice but to abandon their experiment in rebellion. But there is another possibility: the Union and the Confederacy might have come into conflict over any one of several points, and an incident arising therefrom might have precipitated the secession of the upper South. As a matter of fact, not all the secessionist leaders were satisfied with the extent of the Confederacy as it was at the start. Hotheads in South Carolina—and in Virginia too—hoped for a clash that would bring new members to the Confederacy. A couple of the rabid Virginians, Roger A. Pryor and Edmund Ruffin, went to Charleston before the Sumter attack and did all they could to stir up trouble, with the idea that Virginia would go to South Carolina's aid once trouble came. Lincoln, if he had let the Confederacy have its way in April, 1861, would doubtless have had to contend thereafter with a continuation of this deliberate troublemaking.

Thus Lincoln was far less a plotter of war-bringing maneuvers than some of the Confederates themselves. And he was no more the aggressor in the conflict than any of the Confederates were.[7]

The Emancipation Proclamation

Throughout the war, Lincoln repeatedly faced the dilemma of choosing a proper course of action while knowing that no matter which one he chose he would offend someone. Consequently, he often decided not to act at all although this too led him into trouble with men who accused him of being dilatory. On several occasions when Lincoln did act, some men called him an opportunist. Actually he seems to have been simply pragmatic, weighing all decisions against

[7] Richard N. Current, *The Lincoln Nobody Knows* (New York: McGraw-Hill, 1958), pp. 125–129. Copyright © 1958 by Richard N. Current. Used with permission of McGraw-Hill Book Company.

their possible influence on his ultimate goal—saving the Union.

The way in which Lincoln used the slavery issue to the advantage of the North illustrates this. When war began, abolitionists demanded that he invoke his constitutional powers to emancipate the slaves. On the other hand, representatives from the border states insisted that he use those same powers to protect the institution of slavery. Realizing that he could not afford to alienate either of these groups and doubting that the federal government had the constitutional authority to interfere with slavery, Lincoln chose not to act. During the first year of the war he several times overruled and rebuked abolitionist-minded officers who tried to turn the struggle into a war against slavery.

Late in the summer of 1862, however, it seemed to many that the Union might lose the war. In the West, Union armies were stalled in their effort to open the Mississippi, and a Confederate army was beginning a counteroffensive into Kentucky. Things were even worse in the East. The drive to capture Richmond had ended in defeat, the Union was humiliated at the second battle of Bull Run, and Robert E. Lee was preparing to cross the Potomac and invade the North. Moreover, it appeared that England and France were about ready to recognize and aid the Confederacy. Northern spirit and enthusiasm for the war were waning.

Facing this situation, Lincoln recognized two significant facts. First, the most determined sentiment in favor of continuing the war, and aiming for victory at any cost, lay with the antislavery people. Secondly, England and France would not intervene if that meant supporting a side which wished to continue slavery and opposing one which wished to abolish it. They might intervene if the war meant nothing more than a few states attempting to win their independence. But being forced into a position of supporting slavery was something their leaders could not accept.

Having received a public scolding from Horace Greeley in the *New York Tribune* for refusing to free the slaves, Lincoln wrote a reply that was published in many papers. The president's response reflected his pragmatism:

Lincoln's re-election in 1864 prompted this cartoon, "Long Abraham Lincoln a Little Longer."

The New York Public Library

My paramount objective in this struggle *is* to save the Union, and is not either to save or destroy slavery. If I could save the Union without freeing *any* slave, I would do it; and if I could save it by freeing *all* the slaves, I would do it; and if I could do it by freeing some and leaving others alone, I would also do that. What I do about slavery and the colored race, I do because I believe it helps to save this Union. . . . I have here stated my purpose according to my view of *official* duty, and I intend no modification of my oft-expressed *personal* wish that all men, everywhere, could be free.[8]

Viewing the situation late in 1862, Lincoln decided on his course of action and drafted the Emancipation Proclamation. Aware of the significance of timing, he waited for the right moment to publish the document—when Lee's northern invasion had been turned back at the battle of Antietam.

This proclamation was a most unusual document. It had no other legal basis than Lincoln's belief that the president, as commander-in-chief of the armed forces, could adopt any military measure needed to win the war—and the proclamation was offered as just that. It left slavery untouched in those areas controlled by the federal government, and announced abolition only in those places where federal authority was not accepted. In one sense it was among the weakest state papers any president ever issued; yet the proclamation proved to be among the strongest because it changed the whole meaning of the war. It infused the fight with a moral issue, and thus enlisted the driving force of the abolitionists. It deepened the elements of passion and inspiration in the war and rallied liberal thinkers. Furthermore, the proclamation removed the threat of European intervention. This marked a turning point of the war. Lincoln, acting on an almost imperceptible amount of authority, turned what had begun solely as a war to save the Union into a war to end slavery besides.

With the Emancipation Proclamation Lincoln had reversed his policy of two years before. Similarly, while con-

[8] Quoted in Richard Hofstadter, ed., *Great Issues in American History* (New York: Random House, Vintage Books, 1958), 2: 411.

sidering the problems of reconstruction at the end of the war he approved one program for Louisiana, another for Arkansas, and still another for Tennessee. Lincoln was always quick to reject dogmas, labels, and ideologies used by those who attempted to characterize or straitjacket his political philosophy. Consistency meant very little to him. He was concerned with results.

Regardless of what has been said or written about Lincoln, it must not be forgotten that he was an astute politician and that this provided the framework for his achievements as a statesman. And an essential part of his statesmanship was his recognition and insistence that southern people were as much a part of the nation as northerners. He always tried to suppress sectional animosity and reduce the hatred born of war. He never spoke unkindly of the southern people; throughout the war he remained sympathetic toward them.

SUGGESTED READINGS

Current, Richard N. *Lincoln and the First Shot*. Lippincott.

Current, Richard N. *The Lincoln Nobody Knows*. Hill & Wang, American Century Series.

Donald, David. *Lincoln Reconsidered: Essays on the Civil War*. Random House, Vintage Books.

Fehrenbacher, Don. *Prelude to Greatness: Lincoln in the 1850's*. Stanford University Press.

Hofstadter, Richard, ed. *Great Issues in American History*. Vol. 2, *From the Revolution to the Civil War, 1765–1865*. Random House, Vintage Books.

Nevins, Allan. *The Emergence of Lincoln*. 2 vols. Charles Scribner's Sons, Scribner Library.

Nevins, Allan. *The Statesmanship of the Civil War*. Macmillan Co., Collier Books.

Randall, James G. *Mister Lincoln*. Thomas Y. Crowell, Apollo Editions.

Sandburg, Carl. *Abraham Lincoln: The Prairie Years and the War Years*. 3 vols. Dell Books, Laurel Leaf Library.

Stampp, Kenneth. *And the War Came: The North and the Secession Crisis, 1860–1861*. University of Chicago Press, Phoenix Books.

Widows in black walk through the ruined streets of Richmond, Virginia, in 1865.

CHAPTER FIVE

THE CIVIL WAR
AND GETTYSBURG

The beginning of the Civil War in the spring of 1861 ended debate over what to do about secession, and for four years the nation was a battlefield. The Civil War was the greatest emotional experience in the nation's history and the culmination of the most severe crisis it had ever faced. The physical devastation wrought on vast areas was almost incalculable; in Virginia, especially in the Shenandoah Valley, the destruction was nearly complete. Personal fortunes were lost and property destroyed; southern commerce and industry would need decades to rebuild. Although perhaps military necessities, episodes such as General William T. Sherman's march through Georgia from Atlanta to the sea in 1864 left behind not only a wide swath of physical destruction, but also a legacy of bitterness that passed from one southern generation to the next.

Although material losses might be reckoned in dollars, human losses and suffering cannot be. Out of a total population of 33,000,000 people, nearly 600,000 Americans were killed or died from wounds or disease in the Civil War—almost as many as have been lost in all the nation's other wars combined. And there were thousands more who came out of the war permanently maimed in body or in spirit. Allan Nevins regards the Civil War as a terrible tragedy, a blot on the record of our democracy, and a subject for sorrowful regret rather than for the thoughtless

A Boston recruiting office, drawn by a new recruit, Charles Reed, in 1862.

glorification it has sometimes received. In assessing the cost of that conflict, Professor Nevins states:

> . . . We can say that the multitude of Civil War dead represents hundreds of thousands of homes, and hundreds of thousands of families, that might have been, and never were. They represent millions of people who might have been part of our population today and are not. We have lost the books they might have written, the scientific discoveries they might have made, the inventions they might have perfected. Such a loss defies measurement.[1]

Raising the Armies

What induced northern and southern men to join the colors once the war had started? State militia members were in-

[1] Allan Nevins, *The Statesmanship of the Civil War* (New York: Macmillan Co., 1962), p. 153. Copyright © 1953, 1962 by Macmillan Publishing Co., Inc.

structed either to hold themselves in readiness for the president's call or resign, and pride kept most of them from quitting. Many men, usually those who had once been in the regular army, circulated enlistment papers for signatures, which assured them commissions as officers. Early in the war appeals to patriotism, a sense of duty, or the belief in the rightness of the cause were usually sufficient to stimulate enlistments on both sides. One Union volunteer decided to enlist because

the rebels have got right in the path of God and freedom. They refuse to move; let sword and cannon do their mission. Openly or blindly, every Union soldier is doing God's work. Let our foes succeed, and not only will we be draped in mourning, but the best part of humanity will be sharers of our sorrow and despair.[2]

A Confederate soldier wrote that he

dared not refuse to hear the call to arms, so plain was the duty and so urgent the call. His brethren and friends were answering the bugle-call and the roll of the drum. To stay was dishonor and shame.[3]

For those whose sense of duty did not provide sufficient motivation to enlist, there were more subtle encouragements —as noted by one southern volunteer:

The tyranny of public opinion is absolute. No young man able to bear arms *dares* to remain at home: even if the recruiting officers and the conscription law both fail to reach him, he falls under the proscription of the young ladies and *must volunteer*, as I did, though from not quite the same kind of force.[4]

When enthusiasm began to lag, war meetings were or-

[2] Henry T. Johns, *Life with the Forty-Ninth Massachusetts Volunteers* (New York: Ramsey & Bisbee, 1890), pp. 10–11.

[3] Carlton McCarthy, *Detailed Minutiae of Soldier Life in the Army of Northern Virginia* (New York: J. W. Randolph and English, 1888), p. 3.

[4] William G. Stevenson, *Thirteen Months in the Rebel Army* (New York: A. S. Barnes and Burr, 1862), p. 133.

ganized to swell the rolls of volunteers from cities, towns, and rural areas. At such meetings men found it difficult to remain unmoved by the patriotic orations, the stirring music, the emotional appeal of a song urging them to "Rally 'Round the Flag," and the frequent presence on the stage of an old veteran of the War of 1812 or the more recent Mexican War. Each meeting featured a patriotic maiden waving a flag and vowing that she would go "if only she were a man."

> Sometimes the patriotism of such a gathering would be wrought up so intensely by waving banners, martial and vocal music and burning eloquence, that a town's quota would be filled in less than an hour. It needed only the first man to step forward, put down his name, be patted on the back, placed upon the platform and cheered to the echo as the hero of the hour, when a second, a third, a fourth would follow, and at last a perfect stampede set in to sign the enlistment roll. A frenzy of enthusiasm would take possession of the meeting. The complete intoxication of such excitement, like intoxication from liquor, left some of its victims (especially if the fathers of families), on the following day, with sober second thoughts to wrestle with; but Pride, that tyrannical master, rarely let them turn back.[5]

A bounty system was available to town and city officials who experienced difficulty in meeting their quotas of recruits. A typical reaction to this method of recruitment was expressed by a Union soldier in a letter to his family:

> To stimulate volunteering, we have adopted the system of paying bounties to recruits on being mustered into the United States service. A town votes so much bounty to each recruit, expecting that the State will assume the debt as in the case of aid paid to families of soldiers. Those bounties range from $50 to $150, often increased largely by the selfishness or patriotism of private individuals. I suppose no intelligent man really admires this bounty system, yet it has been started, and we must adopt it, or lo! the draft!

[5] Otto Eisenschiml and Ralph Newman, *Eyewitness: The Civil War As We Lived It* (New York: Grosset & Dunlap, 1956), p. 32.

A recruiting office in New York City's Central Park, 1864.

It brings out a good deal of selfishness. Men come from towns where they offer smaller bounties, and enlist where they can secure larger ones. Some carefully conceal physical defects till they are mustered in and paid, and then are discharged for disability, while others desert as soon as they pocket their bounties. Few would object to seeing them receive the full penalty of the law—death![6]

Recruitment was fairly easy during the early months of the war, owing in large part to Union victories in the West. In 1862 General Ulysses S. Grant captured two important Confederate forts, Donelson and Henry, on the lower Tennessee and Cumberland rivers. His Army of the Tennessee then met the Confederates at Shiloh on the east side of the Mississippi River in southern Tennessee. After sustaining a surprise attack and narrowly escaping defeat, Grant's troops stopped the southerners and drove them back.

[6] Johns, *Forty-Ninth Massachusetts*, p. 13.

These victories in the West persuaded Edwin Stanton, who had replaced Simon Cameron as secretary of war, that the Union was winning. He concluded that enough men had volunteered to see the country through the remainder of the conflict. But the Army of the Potomac—the main fighting force in the East—was stopped in its attempt to invade Virginia and capture the Confederate capital, Richmond, early in the summer of 1862. Enthusiasm for enlistment suffered from the combined effects of Stanton's assumption and the Army of the Potomac's military reverses.

On July 1, 1862, President Lincoln called on the governors of the states to supply 300,000 men to serve not six months, the length of previous enlistments, but three years. The response was poor. In August Lincoln appealed for the 300,000 men to serve only nine months, but fewer than 90,000 responded. Early in 1863 Congress was forced to pass a conscription act. Although this initial draft law was far from perfect, it did provide the necessary men to replace those lost through casualties or desertion and to build up the North's military strength.

To provide for a complete military census, the Conscription Act of 1863 divided the North into enrollment districts. Every able-bodied male citizen between the ages of twenty and forty-five, as well as aliens who intended to become citizens, were enrolled as members of the national forces. These men would be subject to service, or drafted, as the government needed them. Each time a new draft was called up, its members were to be divided among the districts according to their military populations. The men called were to be drawn by lot and if a district was able to raise its quota by voluntary enlistments, no draft would be taken from that district. Stanton opposed one feature of the legislation: the provision that a drafted man could either offer a substitute or purchase a discharge for $300.

Men by the thousands filed exemption claims after Lincoln's request in August, 1862. Some said they were physically unfit; others claimed that their religious beliefs would not permit them to fight. Some fled to Canada and others purchased steamship tickets to Europe. The president issued a proclamation stating that "all persons discouraging

Draft rioters looting houses along Lexington Avenue in New York City, 1863.

volunteer enlistments, resisting militia drafts, or guilty of any disloyal practice, affording aid and comfort to Rebels against the authority of the United States" would come under martial law; furthermore, the right of habeas corpus would be suspended for those so charged and held in jail. Despite the proclamation, protests against serving reached serious proportions, especially in the larger cities, after enactment of the national conscription law.

In New York City the first drawing for the draft took place on Saturday, July 12, 1863. The names were printed in the Sunday papers. Many of the draftees listed were immigrants who could ill afford to purchase a discharge or pay for an alternate. When the drawing of names resumed on Monday, a mob invaded the conscription offices and set fire to the building. The offices of the *New York Tribune*, whose editor, Horace Greeley, advocated a vigorous war effort, were raided and set afire. Houses belonging to prominent citizens who supported the administration's war policy were also burned. The assumption that the major purpose of the war was to abolish slavery led some protesters to turn their fury against Negroes, and several blacks were seized and hanged from lamp posts or clubbed to death. By the end of the first day of rioting, the city was in the hands of mobs. Responding to an urgent appeal from city officials, Secretary of War Stanton sent a small force of federal troops to subdue the rioters, and after four days of bloodshed, during which a mob set fire to a Negro orphanage, the soldiers finally restored order.

The effectiveness of the draft in the North can be judged from the following table, taken from official records of the war:

Draft of	1863 July	1864 March 14	1864 July 18	1864 Dec. 19
Number called for	700,000		500,000	300,000
Reduced by credits to	407,092		234,327	300,000
Names drawn	292,441	113,446	231,918	139,024
Failed to report	39,415	27,193	66,159	28,477
Examined	252,566	84,957	138,536	46,128
Exempted for physical disability, etc.	164,855	39,952	82,531	28,631
Exempted by paying commutation	52,288	32,678	1,298	460
Substitutes furnished by registered men	84,733		29,584	12,997
Substitutes furnished by draftees	26,002	8,911	28,502	10,192
Draftees held to personal service	9,881	3,416	26,205	6,845
Voluntary enlistments	489,462		188,172	157,058
Total number obtained	537,672*		272,463	187,092

*The excess, 130,579, credited to call of July 18, 1864.

The Confederate states also conscripted men, and, like the North, the South permitted a man to hire a substitute in order to avoid serving in the army. In addition, the South allowed the exemption of one overseer on each plantation of fifteen or more slaves. Southerners were far from unanimous in their support of the draft law. Some, because of the exemptions the law contained, accused President Jefferson Davis of waging "a rich man's war and a poor man's fight." Others feared conscription would dampen enthusiasm for the war, predicting that the South

Library of Congress

THE VOLUNTARY MANNER IN WHICH SOME OF THE SOUTHERN VOLUNTEERS ENLIST.

A northern view of a southern recruiting office. The objects on the floor, lower right, are "prizes taken by the southern navy."

would surely be defeated if it had to depend on draftees. Many Confederate volunteers had a low opinion of conscripts, as revealed in this letter written by a southern soldier who had been in the army for some time:

> The pride of the volunteers was sorely tried by the incoming of the conscripts—the most despised class in the army —and their devotion to company and regiment was visibly lessened. They could not bear the thought of having these men for comrades, and felt the flag insulted when claimed by one of them as "his flag." It was a great source of annoyance to the true men, but was a necessity. Conscripts crowded together in companies, regiments, and brigades would have been useless, but scattered here and there among the good men, were utilized. And so, gradually, the pleasure that men had in being associated with others whom they respected as equals was seriously marred.[7]

[7] McCarthy, *Detailed Minutiae*, p. 37.

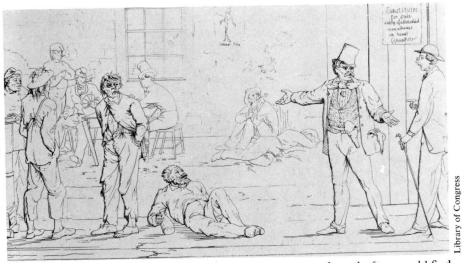

A southern view of a northern "recruiting office," a tavern where draftees could find "Substitutes for sale—supply of able-bodied men always on hand Cheape."

Raising and holding together a Confederate army proved a difficult task for government officials and officers in the field. Desertion reached scandalous proportions, and many southern leaders blamed it for Confederate defeats after 1862; because of it, they said, Confederate generals were unable to follow up successes. During the course of the war, southern armies lost more than 100,000 men this way, with whole companies and regiments sometimes leaving the field at one time. Deserters often hid out in the mountains of the Carolinas or in the swamps of Florida. The number of conscripted replacements barely kept pace with the flow of men leaving the ranks. Many Confederate draftees from areas like eastern Tennessee held Unionist views; others were poor whites who saw the war as a slaveholders' fight to preserve their own privilege and property, not as a fight to save the South. These men usually did not stay in the army long. But ideological considerations probably accounted for fewer desertions than did the day-to-day hardships of the soldier's life—danger, disease, low pay, bad food, lack of warm clothing and shelter, worry over families and farms left behind.

Once in the army, the Civil War soldier in both the

North and the South had to adjust to a new life. There were irksome daily routines, a multitude of unforeseen discomforts, and meals that were poorly prepared, unvarying, and lacking in nourishment. Mail deliveries were infrequent and camp life was monotonous. New acquaintances provided some diversion, and almost without being aware of it, each man developed loyalty to the men he would fight with and to his unit. A Union soldier's letter to his father indicates that he and his comrades took this *esprit de corps* for granted and demanded that every man measure up accordingly:

Old R— was a character in camp. . . . He had been enlisted for our regiment when nearly sixty years of age, by some recruiting officer who ought to have been hung or dismissed from service for such an inhuman act, for it was manifest the poor old man was totally unfit for the service. . . . On every reconnaissance, tour of picket duty, and, in fact, every march, or military service of any nature whatsoever, except ordinary camp guard, he had been unable to perform.

Every morning at surgeon's call, he crept out of his miserable "dugout," and repaired to the hospital to get excused from duty. He spent his days in the dark, gloomy, smoky hole, never leaving it except to "fall in for soup," etc., in which he *failed not*. The army was a cruel place for a sick man, and worse for a man who, by reason of age, incapacity, or disability, still remained about camp, without *performing his share of duty*.

There was little pity, true sympathy, or commiseration, therefore, for the misfortunes of this "non-hewer of wood." The company got "down on him," and from certain men he got nothing but curses and abuse, and by them was dubbed, the "Biled Owl," "Old Hell pestle," etc.

He became thoroughly discouraged at the slow process that promised, at some future date, to release him from this dreadful life. He neglected himself, and sitting over the smoke and ashes of the small fire, which he scarcely manifested enough energy to replenish, his face became pinched, smoke-begrimed, dirty and repulsive; his hair long and tangled and matted. Soon it was discovered that he was alive with vermin, and as the spring approached it became evident that old R— would die from nostalgia or lice unless something was speedily done to set him upon his feet again. A detail was made. He was carried to the creek. His head and face were "lathered and shaved," his clothes stripped from him and burnt, and he was then scrubbed from head to foot with a blacking brush and a new clean change of clothes placed upon him. The metamorphosis was complete, and for a week or so he was quite spruce; but he soon began to relapse into his old ways again, which so disgusted the men, that what ever pity they had entertained before was now changed into positive dislike, which soon found vent in mischief and numberless jokes. Among these smoking him out, by dropping a blanket over the low chimney to his ranch, which always brought him out in the most hasty yet comical manner, crawling on all fours like a crab. His favorite expression was: "Oh! thunder boys,—take k-e-e-er," when his tormentors would set up a roar of laughter.

Another favorite trick on the poor fellow was dropping cartridges down the chimney into his fire. A puff, a dull explosion, and the agility which the old man displayed when he darted out of the low mud doorway of the "shack" was remarkable. Again, watching when he was frying his pork, some deviltry-loving wag would steal up quietly and shake a lot of red pepper down the chimney, part of which going into the fire, and the rest into the fry-pan, down his neck and into his nose, would cause him to splutter, sneeze, and cough, when his tormentors would shout down, "Oh! thunder, you old dead beat, take k-e-e-er!"

The rumor at last came that his discharge papers were at brigade headquarters, and when we moved out, one bright sunny morning, for a tour of picket duty, "Old R—" had scarcely got half a mile from camp, before he stubbed his toe, went down on his knees with his immense *bureau* and load of rations, was ordered back to camp, got his discharge, and we never saw him more.[8]

---

[8] Robert G. Carter, "Four Brothers in Blue," *The Maine Bugle*, 1 October 1898.

U.S. Signal Corps photo

"Federal Troops in Camp," a photograph by Mathew Brady.

To the new recruit, the most difficult thing to endure during his period of training and camp life was the anticipation of battle, an experience so well described in Stephen Crane's novel, *The Red Badge of Courage.* But once having tasted battle, most soldiers became hardened to the presence of destruction and death. This is illustrated by the following letter written early in the war by a Union soldier fighting in the Army of the Potomac as it pushed toward the Confederate capital of Richmond:

> Camp on the Battle Field 6 Miles
> from Richmond Va. June 8th 1862
>
> Friend Lin:
>
> I read yours of the 3rd yesterday was glad to hear from you and will take the first opportunity to answer it. I wrote you some ten days since you will probably hear of the Battle before this reaches you. This was the hardest Battle

we have had yet but we expect a harder one. Every day the men are all in good Spirits as they think the next Battle will be the last. I hope it will and don't care how soon it comes. I think those that are living of us will be in Richmond before next Saturday night. There was a great slaughter here. The line of Battle was some three miles long and the ground was covered some place 4 and 5 deep. In 7 graves there is 64 Rebels all from one Reg. There is a Rebel buried not more than 18 inches from my tent so I have a dead man on one side and a live one on the other. Think the dead one is the least trouble as he don't Snore. When our Reg. arrived here it was dark. The men were tired and laid down in the most convenient place. The next Morning one man found his head between a dead Rebels feet. You may think this is awful but it is nothing after one gets used to it. . . .

Yours Truly
Hollis[9]

Among people on both sides, outpourings of patriotism and an anticipation of glory marked the beginning of the conflict. Northerners and southerners alike were supremely confident at the outset, almost serene in their expectations of swift and total victory. But, for the North especially, the expected successes failed to occur, particularly in the eastern theater, and as the war dragged on and casualties and costs mounted, southern determination seemed to become more steadfast as northern enthusiasm waned. By 1863, after nearly two years of effort, the major Union force—the Army of the Potomac—had failed to achieve any important military objective.

Gettysburg: High-Water Mark of the Confederacy

In November, 1862, Ambrose E. Burnside replaced George B. McClellan as commanding general of the Army of the Potomac. Burnside, better remembered for his luxuriant growth of sidewhiskers than for his military prowess, lost more than 12,000 men the following month at the battle of Fredericksburg. Most of the casualties oc-

[9] Unpublished letter in the collection of Richard H. Brown.

Library of Congress

Lincoln and McClellan on the battlefield at Antietam, 1862.

curred when Burnside ordered a succession of attacks against impregnable Confederate positions commanded by massed artillery. The only Union general to breach the enemy line that December day was George Gordon Meade.

Once again, the Army of the Potomac underwent a change of command. "Fighting Joe" Hooker replaced Burnside, and Hooker's first task was to restore some semblance of morale to the discouraged army. Hooker accomplished this but, notwithstanding all the confidence he displayed, he was not the man to lead the army into battle. At Chancellorsville, in May, 1863, his confidence melted in the face of Robert E. Lee's daring strategy. Hooker let Lee take the initiative, even though his army outnumbered the Confederate forces, and Lee's unorthodox and daring decision to divide his men and, while holding an apparently strong front, to strike the enemy's flank, threw Hooker off balance. Lee drove the Union troops back across the Rappahannock River and won the battle, but at a cost of 13,000 men he could not replace. Worse yet, he lost a general he could hardly do without—Thomas J.

U.S. Signal Corps photo

General Joseph Hooker.

General George Gordon Meade, photographed by Mathew Brady at Gettysburg.

"Stonewall' Jackson. Hooker lost 17,000 men, who were replaced. And so was he. He lost his command to General George Gordon Meade, who observed, "General Hooker has disappointed all his friends by failing to show his fighting qualities at the pinch."[10]

The Union army's spring campaign had failed; the next move appeared to be up to Lee. In a letter written to his wife in June, 1863, General Meade forecast future events accurately:

> Camp near Manassas,
> June 16, 1863
>
> George [General Meade's son, a captain in the Army of the Potomac] wrote to you yesterday and informed you the army had been withdrawn from the Rappahannock. We are now collecting in the vicinity of this place and Centreville, awaiting orders; I presume, also, the development of the enemy's movements. He has not as yet followed us from the Rappahannock, and it is reported that he is in heavy force up the Valley of the Shenandoah. . . . I think Lee has made a mistake in going into Maryland before meeting our army. I hope his movement will arouse the North, and that now men enough will be turned out, not only to drive him back, but to follow and crush him. If his course does not awake the North from the lethargy it has been in, nothing will ever save us. We have had the usual hard service of active operations for the last few days, loss of rest and hard riding. . . .[11]

General Meade's observations proved entirely correct, for Lee had decided to invade the North. Perhaps, Lee thought, carrying the war to the people there would bring about its end, and moving the war out of the South would lift Confederate morale. One more victory against the Union, as decisive as that at Chancellorsville but this time on northern soil, might bring offers of mediation from foreign countries.

A cavalry engagement at Brandy Station in Virginia on

[10] George Gordon Meade, *The Life and Letters of George Gordon Meade*, 2 vols. (New York: Charles Scribner's Sons, 1913), 1: 372.

[11] Ibid., pp. 385–386.

June 9 signaled the movement of Lee's army into the Shenandoah Valley, from which it would launch the invasion across the Potomac, through Maryland, and into Pennsylvania. While still in command of the Union army, General Hooker had been ordered to follow Lee's army northward and stay between it and Washington. Hooker wanted to abandon Harper's Ferry and its arsenal, also in Virginia, and add its garrison of 10,000 men to his army. When his superiors in Washington refused him permission to make this decision, he asked to be relieved of command. On June 28 President Lincoln ordered General Meade to take over the Union army and continue north, trailing Lee.

The following excerpt from a letter Meade wrote to his wife three days before the assignment reveals the politics often involved in such promotions:

I see you are still troubled with visions of my being placed in command. I thought that had all blown over, and I think it has, except in your imagination, and that of some others of my kind friends. I have no doubt great efforts have been made to get McClellan back, and advantage has been taken of the excitement produced by the invasion of Maryland to push his claims; but his friends ought to see that his restoration is out of the question, so long as the present Administration remains in office, and that until they can remove Stanton and Chase, all hope of restoring McClellan is idle. I have no doubt, as you surmise, his friends would look with no favor on my being placed in command. They could not say I was an unprincipled intriguer, who had risen by criticizing and defaming my predecessors and superiors. They could not say I was incompetent, because I have not been tried, and so far as I have been tried I have been singularly successful. They could not say I had never been under fire, because it is notorious no general officer, not even Fighting Joe himself, has been in more battles, or more exposed, than my record evidences. The only thing they can say, and I am willing to admit the justice of the argument, is that it remains to be seen whether I have the capacity to handle successfully a large army. I do not stand, however, any chance, because

I have no friends, political or others, who press or advance my claims or pretensions, and there are so many others who are pressed by influential politicians that it is folly to think I stand any chance upon mere merit alone. Besides, I have not the vanity to think my capacity so pre-eminent, and I know there are plenty of others equally competent with myself, though their names may not have been so much mentioned. For these reasons I have never indulged in any dreams of ambition, contented to await events, and do my duty in the sphere it pleases God to place me in, and I really think it would be as well for you to take the same philosophical view; but do you know, I think your ambition is being roused and that you are beginning to be bitten with the dazzling prospect of having for a husband a commanding general of an army. How is this?[12]

The letter also tells something about the character of the only Union general, aside from Grant, who ever defeated Lee. Lincoln selected Meade because he had a good record and was considered safe and steady, not given to reckless-ness. He apparently had no serious political enemies.

Much has been written about General Robert E. Lee. To the South, he is the greatest of heroes; to West Point, from which he graduated at the top of his class, he is the most distinguished graduate; to his men, he was nearly godlike, as the following description indicates:

I was often at General Lee's headquarters and spoke to him the first time. It is impossible for me to describe the impression he made upon me by his bearing and manners. I felt myself in the presence of a great man, for surely there never was a man upon whom greatness was more stamped. He is the handsomest person I ever saw; every motion an instinct with natural grace, and yet there is a dignity which, while awe-inspiring, makes one feel a sense of confidence and trust that is delightful when it is remem-bered that there are at present so many contingencies de-pendent upon his single will. . . .

Lee . . . does not hesitate to avail himself of some of the

[12] Ibid., pp. 387–389.

This photograph of General Robert E. Lee on his favorite horse, Traveler, was taken
five years after the Confederate defeat at Gettysburg.

aids of material pomp, though perfectly simple in his daily
life, walk and conversation. His favorite horse is a handsome grey called "Traveler," and the General is so fine a
rider that his horse looks like a picture whenever he is
seen. Then Lee wears well-fitted undress grey uniform with
the handsomest trimmings, a handsome sword and cavalry
boots, making him the grandest figure on any field. The
men . . . have for Lee a proud admiration and personal de-

Library of Congress

A cavalry charge at Brandy Station, June 9, 1863, painted by Edwin Forbes.

votion. . . . He is called "Marse Robert" and "Uncle Bob" and whenever seen the men shout and rally around him as their chief for whom they would willingly die."[13]

As was customary in military tactics of the time, Lee planned to use fast-moving cavalry as the eyes and ears of the main body of his army, whose movements were slowed to the rate of the foot soldier and encumbered by endless numbers of supply wagons, caissons, cannons, and ambulances. The battle at Brandy Station on June 9, the largest cavalry engagement up to that time in the war, began when General J.E.B. Stuart's horsemen set out to follow the movements of the Army of the Potomac to gather information for Lee. Stuart's unit ran into Union cavalry led by General Alfred Pleasanton, who was scouting Lee's

[13] Quoted in Susan Leigh Blackford and Charles M. Blackford, eds., *Letters from Lee's Army* (New York: Charles Scribner's Sons, 1947), pp. 114–115.

army. Here Stuart, for the first time in the war, came up against a cavalry force capable of giving him an even fight. The battle was a standoff.

After the clash between Stuart's and Pleasanton's forces, as the Union and Confederate armies maneuvered northward, Lee lost contact with Stuart's cavalry. From that time until the second day of fighting at Gettysburg, the Confederate army operated without the vital knowledge of the opposing army's location, strength, or intentions.

The South's leading cavalry general, James Ewell Brown ("Jeb") Stuart, personified the dash and romanticism of Confederate cavalrymen—a romanticism that was perhaps fed by the novels of Sir Walter Scott. His biographer, Captain John W. Thomason, Jr., described him:

> I sat at the feet of our old men who fought in our War of Southern Confederacy and asked them the questions that boys ask: "What did Stonewall Jackson look like? What sort of a man was Longstreet? A. P. Hill? . . ."
>
> "Well, son"—after deep thought—"Old Stonewall looked —he looked like his pictures. You've seen his pictures. Longstreet, he was a thick-set sort of fellow, with a bushy beard. A. P. Hill was red-headed. . . ." But when you ask about Jeb Stuart, their eyes light up and their faces quicken, and they describe details of his dress, his fighting jacket and his plume—and they hum you songs he loved and tell you how his voice sounded.
>
> . . . There was an elegance about him. He wore gauntlets of white buckskin, and rode in a gray shell jacket, double-breasted, buttoned back to show a close gray vest. His sword, a light French sabre—for he never carried in the Confederate War, the United States Officers' sword of the Old Service—was belted over a cavalry sash of golden silk with tasselled ends. His gray horseman's cloak was lined with scarlet: his wife made it. General Lee, he wrote her, admired it; and he deplored to her the bullet which whipped away its fur collar at Fredericksburg. His horse furniture and equipment were polished leather and bright metal, and he liked to wear a red rose in his jacket when the roses bloomed, and a love-knot of red ribbon when flowers were out of season. His soft, fawn-colored hat was looped up on

Library of Congress

Major General J. E. B. ("Jeb") Stuart.

the right with a gold star, and adorned with a curling os-
trich feather. His boots sported little knightly-spurs of gold—
admiring ladies, even those who never saw him in their
lives, sent him such things. He went conspicuous, all gold
and glitter in the front of great battles and in a hundred
little cavalry fights, which killed men just as dead as
Gettysburg.[14]

Stuart had proposed that his cavalry ride east and to
the rear of the Union troops, raiding their supply wagons
and disrupting their communications with Washington. He
would continue on through Maryland and join the Confederate army north of the Potomac. The plan would slow
the pursuing Union army and permit Lee to reach Pennsylvania and a sound battle position. Lee mulled over the
proposal and passed it on to his second-in-command, General James Longstreet, who had been assigned Stonewall

[14] John W. Thomason, Jr., *Jeb Stuart* (New York: Charles
Scribner's Sons, 1930), pp. 1–2. Copyright 1930 by Charles Scribner's Sons; renewal copyright © 1958 by Leda B. Thomason. Reprinted with permission of Charles Scribner's Sons.

Jackson's command. Longstreet approved. In reading Lee's order to Stuart, however, one might consider how that order should have been interpreted and just what one would have done in Stuart's position:

> June 23, 1863, 5 P.M.
>
> Major-General J.E.B. Stuart, Commanding Cavalry.
> General:
>
> Your notes of 9 and 10:30 A.M. today have just been received. As regards the purchase of tobacco for your men, supposing that Confederate money will not be taken, I am willing for commissaries or quartermasters to purchase this tobacco, and let the men get it from them, but I can have nothing seized by the men. If General Hooker's army [General Meade took command five days after this order] remains inactive you can leave two brigades to watch him, and withdraw the three others, but should he not appear to be moving northward, I think you had better withdraw to this side of the mountains tomorrow night, cross at Shepherdstown next day, and move over to Fredericktown. You will however, be able to judge whether you can pass around their army without hindrance, doing them all the damage you can, and cross the [Potomac] river east of the mountains. In either case, after crossing the river, you must move on and feel the right of [Confederate General Richard] Ewell's troops, collecting information, provisions, etc. Give instructions to the commander of the brigades left behind to watch the flank and rear of the army, and, in the event of the enemy leaving their front, to retire from the mountains west of the Shenandoah, leaving sufficient pickets to guard the passes, and to bring in everything clean along the Valley, closing upon the rear of the Army. . . . Be watchful and circumspect in your movements.
>
> I am very respectfully and truly yours
>
> R. E. Lee, General[15]

Stuart left his two largest brigades to guard the passes of the Shenandoah Valley and took the other three brigades with him. From that time on, no more was heard

---

[15] Quoted in ibid., pp. 422–423.

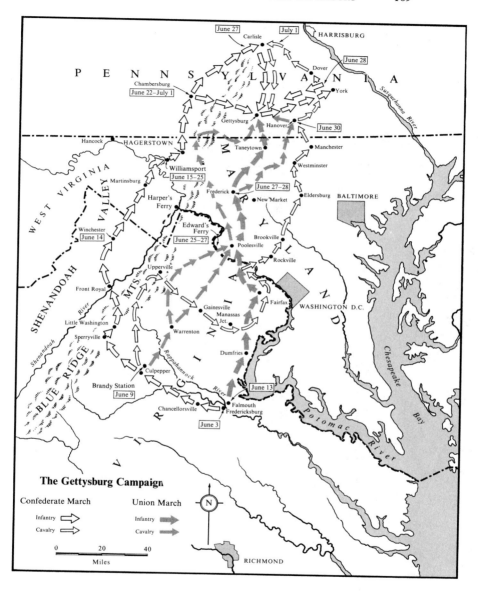

The Gettysburg Campaign

Confederate March   Union March

Infantry   Infantry

Cavalry   Cavalry

0   20   40
Miles

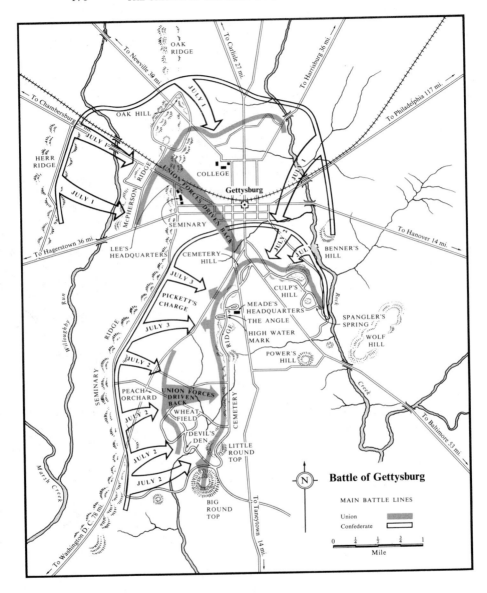

Battle of Gettysburg

MAIN BATTLE LINES

Union
Confederate

from him until he came in from the east to Gettysburg, having ridden completely around the Union army. Stuart's biographer gives full credit to Meade and his Yankee soldiers for winning the battle of Gettysburg, but he also points out:

> It is a principle of the military art, that orders should be clear, direct, and open to that interpretation, only, which the commander desires. Lee's instructions to Stuart do not conform to the principle. They fall outside, even, of that latitude which a general may with propriety extend to a trusted subordinate. Questions affecting vitally the operations of the army are the affair of the commander-in-chief —not any lieutenant, no matter how able. Whatever Stuart's error in judgment, the responsibility lay with Lee, nor, let us add, did Lee in his final report evade it.[16]

Both Lee and Meade had chosen the spots where they intended to fight, but neither of them had planned to make the market town of Gettysburg the scene of the greatest battle of the Civil War. Lee and his generals hurled 75,000 Confederate troops against 97,000 Union troops. For three days, July 1–3, 1863, the battle raged. At its end, 51,000 American soldiers had been killed and wounded. On the first day, Confederates arrived at Gettysburg in great numbers, driving the Union troops out of the town and into defensive positions to the south. The second day the rest of Meade's army arrived, and beat back attempts by Lee to break the northern and southern ends of the Union line. The third day brought the climax—Pickett's famous and futile charge against the center of the Union line.

The First Day

One readable account of the Civil War is Earl Schenck Miers' *Billy Yank and Johnny Reb*. Although the material is fictionalized, it is based on fact. In the following excerpt the narrator is a boy living on a farm near Gettysburg in 1863 who witnessed part of the first day's action.

Fellows who write history books sometimes forget that

[16] Ibid., p. 427.

history happens to everybody—not just to generals and soldiers. Now take me on July 1st, the day the great battle started. That morning a couple of friends and I were picking ripe raspberries along the ridge on Newville road. There we stood, stuffing ourselves, when *boom!*

When that cannon went off, you should have seen us jump—clear over those raspberry bushes—and the way we legged it home, you'd have thought we had been fired from that cannon! When we reached the blacksmith shop, there wasn't one of the customary loafers in sight. "The firing isn't coming this way," I thought. "If we go home, we'll miss the biggest show of our lives!" So the three of us perched on a rail fence near our farm and waited to see what would happen.

Shoes caused the battle of Gettysburg. A Reb general named Henry Heth had tossed all night, worrying over his barefooted soldiers, and with daylight decided he'd come into Gettysburg and find shoes for his boys. Maybe Heth should have known there were Yanks near here, but how could he with Jeb Stuart and the Reb cavalry off in Maryland raiding a Federal wagon train? Jeb should have stuck closer to Lee, for the job of the cavalry is to serve as the "eyes" of an army, but Jeb hadn't, so Heth and his soldiers came swinging down the Chambersburg Pike with shoes and not Yanks on their minds. Outside Gettysburg a mile and a half, rough measure, there's a stream called Willoughby Run. Hills and woods here gave a dandy cover to waiting bluecoats!

From the fence rail we saw it all. Up the road, over the hill, rose the clouds of dust kicked up by Heth and his boys. Wave after wave, on came the Rebs—the sun making the steel gun barrels sparkle. Those gray masses filled the pike and spread over the fields, and still there were more and more. Right there I decided I wasn't waiting to see the whites of their eyes. I flew home.

The house was filled with aunts and girl cousins, all on the point of hysterics. Yet I couldn't much blame 'em with a Reb army swarming over our farm. By the dozens those Rebs stopped to demand something to eat, and through all three days of the battle they never let up on *that!*

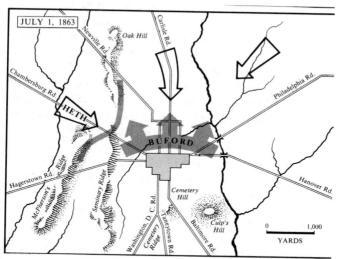

On July 1, Confederate troops drove Buford's Union troops out of the town and into defensive positions to the south.

And what a racket there was over by Willoughby Run. The Yanks had caught Heth, flat-footed. He lost an awful lot of men as prisoners. Yet you can never tell about a battle—you think you're winning and then you discover you're losing. Of course, there has to be a reason, and the answer is usually reinforcements. How General Ewell moved that afternoon, bringing up Alabama troops to bolster Heth's ragged line. An old railroad cut became the center of the toughest fighting as the afternoon wore on! The Rebs got astride that cut, pinning the Yanks into a pocket where the only choice of the Union cannoneers was to blast their way out.

And those Yank gunners did. The water in the buckets beside the big guns looked like ink from the powder smoke. Along the line Yanks reeled and fell. Splinters filled the air like hailstones when Reb bullets hit wheels and axles. Horses plunged, maddened by terror or the pain of wounds. Crash on crash, peal on peal, that's how it went—drivers yelling, shells bursting, bullets hissing, humming and whistling, and Yankee cannon roaring back. But the Rebs were turning our flank. The Yankees were licked and knew it.

They broke and ran like a herd of wild cattle.

Down into Gettysburg they plunged, with the Rebs hot on their heels, banging away. You should have seen the town afterward—streets littered with discarded clothes, blankets, knapsacks, cartridge boxes, dead horses, the bodies of men. Rebs were everywhere, but the Yanks were in the hills beyond the town by then, and the Rebs gave up the chase to celebrate—about the worst mistake any army ever made!

Those Rebs near ruined our farm. Any branch of a cherry tree they could reach, they tore down. We had a flock of about a hundred sheep on a hillside, and the Rebs went after those critters like they had started the war. The Rebs carried away whole carcasses to roast over their fires.[17]

Lieutenant Colonel Arthur James Lyon Fremantle of Her Majesty's Coldstream Guards was on military leave from the British army to observe the Civil War at the time of Gettysburg. Like most Englishmen, Fremantle disliked slavery, but he admired the gallantry and determination of the southerners and chose to observe the war by accompanying the Confederate army. Like most participants in the battle of Gettysburg, Fremantle arrived after much of the first day's fighting was done. It was two o'clock in the afternoon, as he rode with General James Longstreet's corps, when the English officer first became aware of the

... firing [that] became distinctly audible in our front, but although it increased as we progressed, it did not seem to be very heavy.

A spy who was with us insisted upon there being "a pretty tidy bunch of *blue-bellies* in or near Gettysburg," and he declared that he was in their society three days ago.

After passing [General Joseph E.] Johnson's division, we came up to a Florida brigade, which is now in [General A. P.] Hill's corps; but as it had formerly served under Longstreet, the men knew him well. Some of them (after

[17] Earl Schenck Miers, *Billy Yank and Johnny Reb* (Chicago: Rand McNally, 1959), pp. 142–144. Copyright © 1959 by Earl Schenck Miers.

The town of Gettysburg in July, 1863, photographed from Cemetery Hill.

the General had passed) called out to their comrades, "Look out for work now, boys, for here's the old bulldog again."

At 3 P.M. we began to meet wounded men coming to the rear, and the number of these soon increased most rapidly, some hobbling alone, others on stretchers carried by the ambulance corps, and others in the ambulance wagons.

Many of the latter were stripped nearly naked, and displayed very bad wounds. This spectacle so revolting to a person unaccustomed to such sights, produced no impression whatever upon the advancing troops, who certainly go under fire with the most perfect nonchalance. They show no enthusiasm or excitement, but the most complete indifference. This is the effect of two years' almost uninterrupted fighting.

We now began to meet Yankee prisoners coming to the
rear in considerable numbers. Many of them were
wounded, but they seemed already to be on excellent terms
with their captors, with whom they had commenced swap-
ping canteens, tobacco, etc. Among them was a Pennsylvanian colonel, a miserable object from a wound in his
face. In answer to a question, I heard one of them remark,
with a laugh, "We're pretty nigh whipped already." We
next came to a Confederate soldier carrying a Yankee
color, belonging, I think, to a Pennsylvanian regiment,
which he told us he had just captured.

At 4:30 P.M. we came in sight of Gettysburg, and joined
General Lee and General Hill, who were on the top of one
of the ridges which form the peculiar feature of the country
around Gettysburg. We could see the enemy retreating up
one of the opposite ridges, pursued by the Confederates
with loud yells. The position into which the enemy had
been driven was evidently a strong one. His right appeared
to rest on a cemetery, on the top of a high ridge to the
right of Gettysburg, as we looked at it.[18]

Frank Aretas Haskell was an officer on the staff of
Brigadier General John Gibbon, who commanded the
"Iron Brigade"—made up of regiments from several
states—of the Army of the Potomac. General Gibbon later
wrote that Haskell had distinguished himself at Gettysburg
"by his conspicuous coolness and bravery." Within two
weeks after that great battle, Haskell wrote his account of
Gettysburg. What Haskell wrote was not intended to be a
history of the battle but simply his own recollection of
what happened, for he believed that a complete and ac-
curate account of Gettysburg "will never, can never, be
made."

By-and-by, out of the chaos of trash and falsehood that
the newspapers hold, out of the disjointed mass of reports,
out of the traditions and tales that came down from the
field, some eye that never saw the battle will select, and

[18] Arthur J. L. Fremantle and Frank Haskell, *Two Views of
Gettysburg* (Chicago: R. R. Donnelley & Sons, 1964), pp. 39–41.

The Mansell Collection

This sketch by A. R. Waud shows a Union battery in the foreground, with Cemetery Hill, left, and Gettysburg, right, in the distance.

some pen will write, what will be named *the history*. With that the world will be and, if we are alive, we must be, content.[19]

At the same time Fremantle was approaching Gettysburg from the west, Haskell was approaching from the south with General Gibbon's Union troops. Haskell recalled:

. . . It was not long before we began to hear the dull booming of the guns, and as we advanced, from many an eminence or opening among the trees, we could look out upon the white battery smoke, puffing up from the distant field of blood, and drifting up to the clouds. At these sights and sounds, the men looked more serious than before and were more silent, but they marched faster, and straggled less. At

[19] Ibid., pp. 247–248.

about five o'clock P.M., as we were riding along at the head
of the column, we met an ambulance, accompanied by two
or three mounted officers—we knew them to be staff officers of Gen. [John F.] Reynolds. Their faces told plainly
enough what load the vehicle carried—it was the dead body
of Gen. Reynolds. Very early in the action, while seeing
personally to the formation of his lines under fire, he was
shot through the head by a musket or rifle bullet, and
killed almost instantly. His death at this time affected us
much, for he was one of the soldier Generals of the army,
a man whose soul was in his country's work, which he did
with a soldier's high honor and fidelity. . . .

. . . Late in the afternoon as we came near the field,
from some slightly wounded men we met, and occasional
stragglers from the scene of operations in front, we got
many rumors, and much disjointed information of battle,
of lakes of blood, of rout and panic and undescribable dis-
aster, from all of which the narrators were just fortunate
enough to have barely escaped, the sole survivors. These
stragglers are always terrible liars![20]

The cannonading that Fremantle and Haskell heard and
the wounded and the straggling soldiers they saw were
coming from the vicinity of McPherson Ridge, just northwest of Gettysburg. The most vicious and bloody fighting
of the first day centered on a railroad cut in that low ridge.
Union cannoneer Augustus Buell described that action:

The day was very hot, many of the boys had their jackets
off, and they exchanged little words of cheer with one another as the gray line came on. In quick, sharp tones, like

[20] Ibid., pp. 107–108, 109. Major General John Reynolds was
among the Union's most able officers. He had been offered command of the army earlier but had refused because he believed that
the War Department would not permit him a free hand. After
Reynolds' death, the First Infantry Corps was commanded by
General Abner Doubleday, a crusty New Englander who had good
cause for his intense dislike of southerners. Doubleday had been
second-in-command at Fort Sumter when it was attacked in 1861.
While stationed at Charleston before the attack, Doubleday had
had to endure the malevolence South Carolinians exhibited toward
Yankee soldiers. Doubleday has been credited with developing the
rules for baseball.

Library of Congress

The field where General Reynolds fell on the first day of the battle.

successive reports of a repeating rifle, came our captain's orders: "Load . . . Canister . . . Double!" There was a hustling of cannoneers, a few thumps of the rammer heads, and then "Ready! . . . By piece! . . . At will! . . . Fire!"

Directly in our Front the Rebel infantry had been forced to halt and lie down, by the tornado of canister that we had given them. But the regiments to their right kept on, as if to cut us off from the rest of our troops.

Then ensued probably the most desperate fight ever waged between artillery and infantry at close range without a particle of cover on either side. They gave us volley after volley in front and flank, and we gave them double canister as fast as we could load. The 6th Wisconsin and the 11th Pennsylvania men crawled up over the bank of the cut and joined their musketry to our canister.

The years have but softened in memory the picture of our burly corporal, bareheaded, his hair matted with blood from a scalp wound, and wiping the crimson fluid out of his eyes to sight the gun; of the steady orderly sergeant, moving calmly from gun to gun, now and then changing men about as one after another was hit and fell, stooping over a wounded man to help him up, or aiding another to stagger to the rear; of the dauntless commanding officer on foot among the guns, cheering the men, praising this one and that one, and ever and anon profanely exhorting to us to "feed it to 'em!" . . .

For a few moments the whole Rebel line seemed to waver, and we thought that maybe we could repulse them singlehanded. But their lines came steadily on. Orders were given to limber to the rear, the 6th Wisconsin and the 11th Pennsylvania behind us having begun to fall back down the railroad track toward the town, turning about and firing as they retreated.

The Rebels could have captured or destroyed our battery if they had made a sharp rush. But their general [Heth] has told me since the war that they were not able to conceive that a battery would hold such a position so long without adequate infantry support and were convinced that the railroad cut behind us must be full of concealed infantry.

We got off by the skin of our teeth and before sundown were in position on the north brow of Cemetery Hill.[21]

Lee arrived at three in the afternoon and witnessed the Union retreat through Gettysburg. Through his fieldglasses, he watched the Union re-establish its lines on Cemetery Ridge south of town. General Meade reached the battlefield early on the morning of the second day. General Oliver O. Howard, who along with General Winfield S. Hancock had rallied the Union troops along Cemetery Ridge, rode along the Union line with General Meade and told him: "I am confident that we can hold this position."

"I am glad to hear you say so," answered Meade, "for it is too late to leave it."

The Second Day

The second day at Gettysburg found the two opposing

[21] Quoted in Eisenschiml and Newman, *Eyewitness*, pp. 470–471.

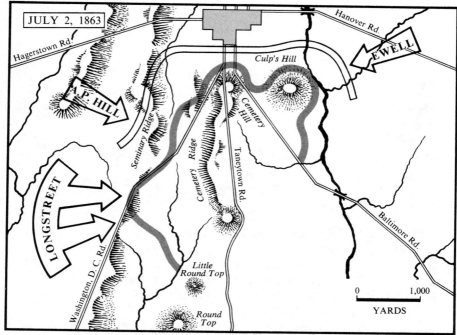

On the second day, Confederate troops under Generals Longstreet, Hill, and Ewell attacked the northern and southern ends of the Union line, but the Union troops— now reinforced by the remainder of General Meade's army—were able to hold both Round Tops and establish themselves more securely along Cemetery Ridge.

armies facing each other across level ground between two ridges. Lee's Confederates occupied Seminary Ridge— named after a Lutheran seminary on the ridge just west of Gettysburg. About a mile east of there, Meade's Union troops strung out along Cemetery Ridge.

What do men do in those last hours before a great battle begins? Frank Haskell, in a position along Cemetery Ridge just south of Meade's headquarters, described the Union activity:

> The day wore on, the weather still sultry, and the sky overcast, with a mizzling effort at rain. When the audience has all assembled, time seems long until the curtain rises; so today. "Will there be a battle today?" "Shall we attack the Rebel?" "Will he attack us?" These and similar questions, later in the morning, were thought or asked a million times.

A Confederate soldier, dead or perhaps only sleeping, at Gettysburg. An average of 430 soldiers died every day during the four years of the Civil War.

Library of Congress

Meanwhile, on our part, all was put in the last state of readiness for battle. Surgeons were busy riding about selecting eligible places for Hospitals, and hunting streams, and springs, and wells. Ambulances, and ambulance men, were brought up near the lines, and stretchers gotten ready for use. Who of us could tell but that he would be the first to need them? The Provost Guards were busy driving up stragglers, and causing them to join their regiments. Ammunition wagons were driven to suitable places, and pack mules bearing boxes of cartridges; and the commands were informed where they might be found. Officers were sent to see that the men had each his hundred rounds of ammunition. Generals and their Staffs were riding here and there among their commands to see that all was right. A staff officer, or an orderly might be seen galloping furiously in the transmission of some order or message. All, all was ready—and yet the sound of no gun had disturbed the air or ear today.

And so the men stacked their arms—in long bristling rows they stood along the crests—and were at ease. Some men of the Second and Third Corps pulled down the rail fences near—and piled them up for breastworks in their front. Some loitered, some went to sleep upon the ground, some, a single man carrying twenty canteens slung over his shoulder, went for water. Some made them a fire and boiled a dipper of coffee. Some with knees cocked up, enjoyed the soldier's peculiar solace, a pipe of tobacco. Some were mirthful and chatty, and some were serious and silent.[22]

Not all of Meade's forces had reached the field, and Lee wanted to attack the Union positions before that happened. Delays, however, postponed action until late in the afternoon. Lee's attacks were to be aimed at Cemetery Hill and Culp's Hill, just east of the hooklike end of Cemetery Ridge, on the Union right, and at Little Round Top on the Union left. The coordinated attacks could have turned either flank of the Union line or severed it at either point.

General Longstreet, who had unsuccessfully urged Lee to fight a defensive battle, was to lead the Confederate attack on one of the Union positions. Colonel Fremantle described the action from the southern viewpoint:

At 2 P.M. General Longstreet advised me, if I wished to have a good view of the battle, to return to my tree of yesterday [Fremantle had viewed the previous day's action perched in a tree]. I did so, and remained there . . . during the rest of the afternoon. But until 4:45 P.M. all was profoundly still, and we began to doubt whether a fight was coming off today at all.

At that time, however, Longstreet suddenly commenced a heavy cannonade on the right. Ewell [commanding the Confederate troops attacking the Union right] immediately took it up on the left. The enemy replied with at least equal

[22] Fremantle and Haskell, *Two Views*, pp. 122–124.

fury, and in a few moments the firing along the whole line was as heavy as it is possible to conceive. A dense smoke arose for six miles. There was little wind to drive it away, and the air seemed full of shells—each of which appeared to have a different style of going, and to make a different noise from the others. The ordnance on both sides is of a very varied description.

Every now and then a caisson would blow up—if a Federal one, a Confederate yell would immediately follow. The Southern troops, when charging, or to express their delight, always yell in a manner peculiar to themselves. The Yankee cheer is much more like ours; but the Confederate officers declare that the Rebel yell has a particular merit, and always produces a salutary and useful effect upon their adversaries. A corps is sometimes spoken of as a "good yelling regiment."

As soon as the firing began, General Lee joined [General A. P.] Hill just below our tree, and he remained there nearly all the time, looking through his fieldglass—sometimes talking to Hill and sometimes to Colonel [A. L.] Long of his staff. But generally he sat quite alone on the stump of a tree. What I remarked especially was, that during the whole time the firing continued, he only sent one message, and only received one report. It is evidently his system to arrange the plan thoroughly with the three corps commanders, and then leave to them the duty of modifying and carrying it out to the best of their abilities.

When the cannonade was at its height, a Confederate band of music, between the cemetery and ourselves, began to play polkas and waltzes, which sounded very curious, accompanied by the hissing bursting of the shells.[23]

General Dan Sickles of the Union's Third Corps was supposed to have secured the southern part of the Union line, from Cemetery Ridge along the base of Little Round Top to Big Round Top. But, without orders from Meade, he moved his line down to the Emmitsburg road, where his men were spread through a peach orchard, and then moved back through Devil's Den, a jumbled area of rocks and

[23] Ibid., pp. 46–48.

Library of Congress

The Union defense of Cemetery Hill on the second day of the battle.

boulders at the base of Little Round Top, which he had failed to secure. General G. K. Warren hurried Union troops to the top of this commanding position just ahead of the charging Confederates. As Sickles' men moved down from Cemetery Ridge to the position just described, Frank Haskell looked on in dismay.

Somewhat after one o'clock P.M.—the skirmish firing had nearly ceased now—a movement of the Third Corps occurred, which I shall describe. I cannot conjecture the reason of this movement. From the position of the Third Corps, as I have mentioned, to the second ridge West, the distance is about a thousand yards, and there the Emmitsburg road runs near the crest of the ridge. General Sickles commenced to advance his whole Corps, from the general line, straight to the front . . . along, and near the road. What his purpose could have been is past conjecture. It was not ordered by General Meade, as I heard him say, and he disapproved of it as soon as it was made known to him. Generals Hancock and Gibbon, as they saw the move in progress, criticized its propriety sharply, as I know, and foretold quite accurately what would be the result.

. . . This move of the Third Corps was an important one—it developed the battle. . . . Oh!, if this Corps had kept its strong position upon the crest, and supported by the rest of the army, had waited for the attack of the enemy!

. . . As the enemy opened upon Sickles with his batteries, some five or six in all, I suppose, firing slowly, Sickles with as many replied, and with much more spirit. The artillery fire became quite animated, soon; but the enemy was forced to withdraw his guns farther and farther away, and ours advanced upon him. It was not long before the cannonade ceased altogether, the enemy having retired out of range, and Sickles, having temporarily halted his command, pending this, moved forward again to the position he desired, or nearly that. It was now about five o'clock . . . we hear more artillery firing upon Sickles' left—the enemy seems to be opening again, and as we watch the Rebel batteries seem to be advancing there. The cannonade is soon opened again and with great spirit upon both sides. The enemy's batteries press those of Sickles, and pound the shot upon them, and this time they in turn begin to retire to a position nearer the infantry. The enemy seems to be fearfully in earnest this time. And what is more ominous than the thunder or the shot of his advancing guns, this time, in the intervals between his batteries, far to Sickles' left, appear the long lines and the columns of the Rebel infantry, now unmistakably moving out to the attack. The position of the Third Corps becomes at once one of great peril, and it is probable that its commander by this time began to realize his true situation.[24]

For more than an hour, Haskell and the other men on Cemetery Ridge observed the Third Corps' predicament. The fighting enveloped the peach orchard, the wheatfield, Devil's Den, and the Round Tops themselves. Sickles was carried from the field, minus one leg. Then Haskell and the Second Corps were caught up. At a great loss of men, the Union troops finally drove the Confederates back from the peach orchard below Cemetery Ridge and from the ridge itself.

Longstreet's forces were unable to take Little Round

[24] Ibid., pp. 131–132, 134.

Top, but they did drive the Union soldiers from Culp's Hill. Darkness finally put an end to the second day of fighting.

The Third Day

Lee had tried to turn the Union flanks and had failed. On the morning of the third day not only was the Union line still intact but it was also strengthened by arrivals of fresh infantry and new batteries. Facing Lee on that day was the entire Army of the Potomac, and a successful Union assault on Culp's Hill drove the Confederates off.

General Longstreet wanted Lee to move to the right of Meade's army and maneuver the Union officers into attacking. Lee pointed to Cemetery Ridge and replied, "The enemy is there, and I am going to strike him." Lee planned a massive frontal assault on the center of the Union line with General G. E. Pickett's division, which had not yet taken part in the battle. Longstreet disagreed with the plan, for he thought the Union position much too strong to take, but he followed Lee's orders to prepare Pickett's men for the assault that was to follow an artillery barrage. Long-

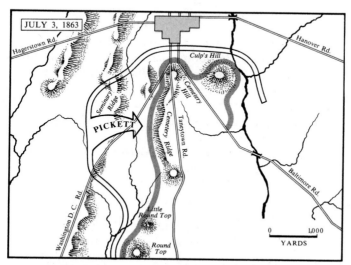

The third day of the battle brought Pickett's fatal charge against the center of the Union line.

street, however, was so convinced of the hopelessness of the attempt that he could not himself give the order to attack. He requested Colonel E. P. Alexander, commanding the Confederate artillery, to notify Pickett when he thought the time was right for the infantry assault.

At 1:00 P.M., the signal guns were fired and cannonading by 172 Confederate guns began. The Union line answered with 220 guns firing all along a two-mile front. The effects of the bombardments were devastating. A reporter for the *New York Herald* wrote:

> A flock of pigeons were scarcely thicker than the flock of horrible missiles that now descended on our position. The storm broke upon us so suddenly that soldiers and officers died, some with cigars between their teeth, some with pieces of food in their fingers, and one with a miniature of his sister in his hands. Horses fell, shrieking awful cries. The boards of fences flew in splinters through the air. The earth, torn up in clouds, blinded the eyes of hurrying men. As I groped for the shelter of the bluff, an old private was struck scarcely ten feet away by a cannon ball, which tore through him, extorting such a low, intense cry of mortal pain as I pray to God I may never again hear.[25]

After nearly two hours, the cannonading died away. The assault column of 15,000 Confederates, arrayed in ranks, was spread out for nearly a mile. Its primary objective was a small copse of trees in front of which was a low stone wall. This wall was to become the high-water mark of the Confederacy, for here it reached its crest and receded. One hundred fifty men of the 15,000 made it beyond, only to be killed or captured. The remainder were killed, wounded, or driven back to the Confederate lines.

Just minutes before leading the assualt, General Pickett penciled a note to his sweetheart:

> A summons came from Old Peter [General Longstreet]. . . . I have never seen [him] so grave and troubled. For several minutes after I had saluted him he looked at me without speaking. Then in an agonized voice, the reserve

[25] Quoted in Eisenschiml and Newman, *Eyewitness*, p. 493.

all gone, he said, "Pickett, I am being crucified. I have instructed Alexander to give you your orders, for I can't."

While he was yet speaking, a note was brought to me from Alexander. After reading it I handed it to Pete, asking if I should obey and go forward. He looked at me for a moment, then held out his hand. Presently, clasping his other hand over mine without speaking, he bowed his head on his breast. I shall never forget the look in his face nor the clasp of his hand, and I saw tears glistening on his cheeks and beard. The stern old war horse, God bless him, was weeping for his men and, I know, praying too that this cup might pass from them. It is almost three o'clock.[26]

As the first of the Confederates approached the low stone wall the defenders broke, and it was Frank Haskell who rallied these men back to the wall where they threw back the assault. Probably no other description of Pickett's charge is as vivid or authentic as Haskell's, of which this is a small portion:

None on that crest now need to be told that *the enemy is advancing.* Every eye could see his legions, an overwhelming resistless tide of an ocean of armed men sweeping upon us! Regiment after regiment, and brigade after brigade move from the woods and readily take their places in the lines forming the assault. . . . More than half a mile their front extends; more than a thousand yards the dull gray masses deploy, man touching man, rank pressing rank, and line supporting line. The red flags wave, their horsemen gallop up and down; the arms of eighteen thousand men, barrel and bayonet, gleam in the sun, a sloping forest of flashing steel. Right on they move, as with one soul, in perfect order, without impediment of ditch, or wall or stream, over ridge and slope, through orchard and meadow, and cornfield, magnificent, grim, irresistible.

All was orderly and still upon our crest; no noise and no confusion. The men had little need of commands, for the survivors of a dozen battles knew well enough what this array in front portended, and, already in their places, they would be prepared to act when the right time should come.

[26] Quoted in ibid., p. 492.

The click of the locks as each man raised the hammer to feel with his finger that the cap was on the nipple; the sharp jar as a musket touched a stone upon the wall when thrust in aiming over it, and the clicking of the iron axles as the guns were rolled up by hand a little further to the front, were quite all the sounds that could be heard. Cap-boxes were slid around to the front of the body; cartridge boxes opened, officers opened their pistol-holsters. With such preparations, little more was needed. . . .

General Gibbon rode down the lines, cool and calm, and in an unimpassioned voice he said to the men, "Do not hurry, men, and fire too fast, let them come up close before you fire, and then aim low and steadily." . . .

Our skirmishers open spattering fire along the front, and, fighting, retire upon the main line—the first drops, the heralds of the storm, sounding on our windows. Then the thunder of our guns . . . shake and reverberate again through the air, and their sounding shells smite the enemy. . . . All our available guns are now active, and from the fire of shells, as the range grows shorter and shorter, they change to shrapnel, and from shrapnel to canister, but in spite of shells, and shrapnel and canister, without wavering or halt, the hardy lines of the enemy continue to move on. . . .

And so across all that broad open ground they have come, nearer and nearer, nearly half the way, with our guns bellowing in their faces, until now a hundred yards, no more, divide our ready left from their advancing right. The eager men there are impatient to begin. Let them . . . . [The Confederates are finally driven back and now the Union] line springs—the crest of the solid ground with a great roar, heaves forward its maddened load, men, arms, smoke, fire, a fighting mass. It rolls to the wall—flash meets flash, the wall is crossed—a moment ensues of thrusts, yells, blows, shots, and undistinguishable conflict, followed by a shout universal that makes the welkin [the sky] ring again, and the last and bloodiest fight of the great battle of Gettysburg is ended and won.[27]

[27] Fremantle and Haskell, *Two Views*, pp. 189–190, 191, 203–204.

The Army of the Potomac, under an able leader, had defeated the Army of Northern Virginia, which now slowly retreated southward. Meade consulted with his generals and five out of the eight counseled him not to pursue Lee. He did not, and for this Meade was severely criticized.

Allan Nevins has advised anyone tempted to think of Gettysburg only in terms of heroic episodes, color, and drama to turn to the pages of the book *Battles and Leaders*, in which General John D. Imboden described the removal of Confederate wounded back to Maryland.

> For four hours I hurried forward on my way to the front, and in all that time I was never out of hearing of the groans and cries of the wounded and dying. Scarcely one in a hundred had received adequate surgical aid, owing to the demands on the hard-working surgeons from still worse cases that had to be left behind. Many of the wounded in their wagons had been without food for thirty-six hours. Their torn and bloody clothing, matted and hardened, was rasping the tender, inflamed, and still oozing wounds. Very few of the wagons had even a layer of straw in them, and all were without springs. The road was rough and rocky from the heavy washings of the preceding day. The jolting was enough to have killed strong men, if long exposed to it. From nearly every wagon as the teams trotted on, urged by whip and shout, came such cries and shrieks as these:
>
> "My God! Why can't I die?"
>
> "My God! Will no one have mercy and kill me?"
>
> "Stop! Oh, for God's sake stop just for one minute; take me out and leave me to die on the roadside."
>
> Occasionally a wagon would be passed from which only low, deep moans could be heard. No help could be rendered to any of the sufferers. No heed could be given to any of their appeals. Mercy and duty to the many forbade the loss of a moment in the vain effort then and there to comply with the prayers of the few. On! On! We must move on. The storm continued and the darkness was appalling. There was no time even to fill a canteen with water for a dying man; for, except the drivers and the guards, all were wounded and utterly helpless in that vast procession of misery.

The retreat of Lee's army in the rain, painted by Edwin Forbes.

During this one night I realized more of the horrors of war than I had in all the preceding two years.[28]

Aftermath of Gettysburg

The defeat at Gettysburg in the East was compounded by the fall of Vicksburg in the West on the same day that Lee withdrew his beaten army from Seminary Ridge. "The Father of Waters again goes unvexed to the sea," observed Lincoln, "Thanks to all. For the great Republic—for the principle it lives by and keeps alive—for man's vast future —thanks to all." The South was defeated. It would be another year and nine months before it surrendered, after thousands more lives were lost, after untold additional destruction in such places as Chickamauga, Atlanta, Cold Harbor, Columbia, Petersburg, and Richmond itself. Union victories at Gettysburg ended southern hopes of foreign intervention. The building of ships in England and France for the Confederates came to an abrupt halt.

On November 19, 1863, at the dedication of the Union Cemetery at Gettysburg, President Lincoln offered a few words on the significance of the Gettysburg battleground. Lincoln's speech was delivered quickly—it had followed a

[28] Quoted in Nevins, *Statesmanship*, pp. 148–149.

lengthy address by one of the nation's most distinguished orators—and most of those present could not hear the words. Indeed, photographers complained that Lincoln got up, said his say, and sat down before they could get their cameras set up. There was little immediate reaction to Lincoln's speech in the public press. But it is ironic that this speech, in which Lincoln asserts that everyone will soon forget the speechmaking but never forget the valor of the Union and Confederate dead, has grown steadily in fame and significance, whereas the battle itself has tended to become merely a name and a vagueness.

Fourscore and seven years ago our fathers brought forth on this continent, a new nation, conceived in liberty, and dedicated to the proposition that all men are created equal.

Now we are engaged in a great civil war, testing whether that nation, or any nation so conceived and so dedicated, can long endure. We are met on a great battlefield of that war. We have come to dedicate a portion of that field, as a final resting-place for those who here gave their lives that that nation might live. It is altogether fitting and proper that we should do this.

But, in a larger sense, we cannot dedicate—we cannot consecrate—we cannot hallow—this ground. The brave men, living and dead, who struggled here, have consecrated it, far above our poor power to add or detract. The world will little note, nor long remember what we say here, but it can never forget what they did here. It is for us the living, rather, to be dedicated here to the unfinished work which they who fought here have thus far so nobly advanced. It is rather for us to be here dedicated to the great task remaining before us—that from these honored dead we take increased devotion to that cause for which they gave the last full measure of devotion—that we here highly resolve that these dead shall not have died in vain—that this nation, under God, shall have a new birth of freedom—and that government of the people, by the people, and for the people, shall not perish from the earth.

SUGGESTED READINGS

Blackford, Susan L., and Blackford, Charles M., eds. *Letters from Lee's Army*. A. S. Barnes.

Catton, Bruce. *Mr. Lincoln's Army*. Simon & Schuster, Pocket Books.

Catton, Bruce, ed. *American Heritage Short History of the Civil War*. Dell Books, Laurel Leaf Library.

Crane, Stephen. *The Red Badge of Courage*. Macmillan Co., Collier Books.

Eaton, Clement. *History of the Southern Confederacy*. Free Press.

Eisenschiml, Otto. *The Hidden Face of the Civil War*. Bobbs-Merrill, Charter Books.

Haskell, Frank Aretas. *The Battle of Gettysburg*. Edited by Bruce Catton. Houghton Mifflin, Sentry Editions.

Lord, Walter, ed. *The Fremantle Diary: The South at War*. G. P. Putnam's Sons, Capricorn Books.

Miers, Earl Schenck. *The Emergence of the American Conscience from Sumter to Appomattox*. Macmillan Co., Collier Books.

Miers, Earl Schenck. *Robert E. Lee*. Harper & Row, Perennial Library.

Miers, Earl Schenck, ed. *The General Who Marched to Hell: William Tecumseh Sherman*. Macmillan Co., Collier Books.

Newman, Ralph, and Long, E. B. *Civil War Digest*. Grosset & Dunlap, Universal Library.

BIBLIOGRAPHY

Chapter One

Beale, Howard K. "What Historians Have Said About the Causes of the Civil War." In *Theory and Practice in Historical Study*. New York: Social Science Research Council, 1945.

Channing, Edward. *A History of the United States*. Vol. 6. New York: Macmillan Co., 1925.

Cole, Arthur. *The Irrepressible Conflict, 1850–1865*. New York: Macmillan Co., 1934.

Craven, Avery O. *The Coming of the Civil War*. Chicago: University of Chicago Press, 1950.

Freehling, William. *Prelude to Civil War: The Nullification Controversy in South Carolina, 1816–1836*. New York: Harper & Row, 1968.

Freeman, Douglas Southall. *Robert E. Lee: A Biography*. Vol. 1. New York: Charles Scribner's Sons, 1934.

Lindsey, David. *Americans in Conflict: The Civil War and Reconstruction*. Boston: Houghton Mifflin, 1974.

Nevins, Allan. *The Ordeal of the Union*. 2 vols. New York: Charles Scribner's Sons, 1947.

Pressly, Thomas. *Americans Interpret Their Civil War*. Princeton: Princeton University Press, 1961.

Rhodes, James F. *History of the United States from the Compromise of 1850 to the McKinley-Bryan Campaign of 1896*. 8 vols. Port Washington, N.Y.: Kennikat Press, 1896–1920.

Rozwenc, Edwin. *The Causes of the American Civil War*. Boston: D. C. Heath, 1961.

Stampp, Kenneth, ed. *The Causes of the Civil War*. Englewood Cliffs, N.J.: Prentice-Hall, 1959.

Chapter Two

Cash, W. J. *The Mind of the South.* New York: Alfred A. Knopf, 1941.

Current, Richard N. *John C. Calhoun.* New York: Washington Square Press, 1963.

De Tocqueville, Alexis. *Democracy in America.* New York: New American Library, 1963.

De Voto, Bernard. *Across the Wide Missouri.* Boston: Houghton Mifflin, 1964.

Eaton, Clement. *A History of the Old South.* New York: Macmillan Co., 1966.

Furnas, J. C. *The Americans: A Social History of the United States.* New York: G. P. Putnam's Sons, 1969.

Grantham, D. W., ed. *The South and the Sectional Image.* New York: Harper & Row, 1967.

Horgan, Paul. *Great River: The Rio Grande in North American History.* 2 vols. New York: Holt, Rinehart & Winston, 1954.

O'Dea, Thomas. *The Mormons.* Chicago: University of Chicago Press, 1964.

Olmsted, Frederick Law. *The Slave States Before the Civil War.* New York: G. P. Putnam's Sons, 1959.

Padover, Saul K. *The Genius of America.* New York: McGraw-Hill, 1960.

Rothe, Bertha, ed. *The Daniel Webster Reader.* New York: Oceana, 1956.

Stampp, Kenneth. *And the War Came: The North and the Secession Crisis, 1860–1861.* Baton Rouge: Louisiana State University Press, 1950.

Stampp, Kenneth, ed. *The Causes of the Civil War.* Englewood Cliffs, N.J.: Prentice-Hall, 1959.

Taylor, William. *Cavalier and Yankee.* New York: Braziller, 1961.

Tryon, Warren S., ed. *My Native Land: Life in America, 1790–1870.* Chicago: University of Chicago Press, 1952.

Turner, Frederick Jackson. *The United States, 1830–1850.* New York: Holt, Rinehart & Winston, 1965.

Woodham-Smith, Cecil. *The Great Hunger.* New York: Harper & Row, 1962.

Woodward, C. Vann. *The Burden of Southern History*. New York: Random House, Vintage Books, 1960.

Chapter Three

Barnes, Gilbert. *The Antislavery Impulse: 1830–1844*. New York: Harcourt, Brace & World, 1964.

Bennett, Lerone, Jr. *Before the Mayflower: A History of Black America*. Rev. ed. Chicago: Johnson Publishing Co., 1969.

Botkin, Benjamin A., ed. *Lay My Burden Down: A Folk History of Slavery*. Chicago: University of Chicago Press, 1961.

Davis, David. *The Problem of Slavery in Western Culture*. Ithaca, N.Y.: Cornell University Press, 1966.

Dumond, Dwight L. *Antislavery: The Crusade for Freedom in America*. New York: W. W. Norton, 1966.

Elkins, Stanley M. *Slavery: A Problem in American Institutional and Intellectual Life*. Chicago: University of Chicago Press, 1959.

Fogel, Robert W., and Engerman, Stanley L. *Time on the Cross: The Economics of American Negro Slavery*. Boston: Little, Brown, 1974.

Franklin, John Hope. *From Slavery to Freedom: A History of American Negroes*. New York: Alfred A. Knopf, 1967.

Genovese, Eugene D. "American Slaves and Their History." *The New York Review of Books* 15, no. 10 (December 3, 1970): 34–43.

Genovese, Eugene D. *The Political Economy of Slavery: Studies in the Economy and Society of the Slave South*. New York: Random House, Vintage Books, 1965.

Genovese, Eugene D. *Roll, Jordan, Roll: The World the Slaves Made*. New York: Pantheon Books, 1974.

McKitrick, Eric L., ed. *Slavery Defended: The Views of the Old South*. Englewood Cliffs, N.J.: Prentice-Hall, 1963.

Phillips, Ulrich B. *American Negro Slavery*. New York: D. Appleton & Co., 1918.

Quarles, Benjamin, and Stuckey, Sterling, eds. *A People Uprooted, 1500–1800*. Vol. 1, Afro-American History

Series. Chicago: Encyclopaedia Brittanica Educational Corp., 1969.

Stampp, Kenneth. *The Peculiar Institution.* New York: Alfred A. Knopf, 1956.

Thomas, John L. *The Liberator: William Lloyd Garrison.* Boston: Little, Brown, 1963.

Thomas, John L., ed. *Slavery Attacked: The Abolitionist Crusade.* Englewood Cliffs, N.J.: Prentice-Hall, 1964.

Wade, Richard C. *Slavery in the Cities: The South, 1820–1860.* New York: Oxford University Press, 1964.

Wish, Harvey, ed. *Ante-Bellum.* New York: G. P. Putnam's Sons, 1960.

Woodman, Harold. "The Profitability of Slavery, a Historical Perennial." *The Journal of Southern History* 29 (1963): 303–325.

Chapter Four

Current, Richard N. *The Lincoln Nobody Knows.* New York: McGraw-Hill, 1958.

Donald, David. *Lincoln Reconsidered: Essays on the Civil War.* New York: Random House, Vintage Books, 1956.

Fehrenbacher, Don. *Prelude to Greatness: Lincoln in the 1850's.* Palo Alto, Calif.: Stanford University Press, 1962.

Hofstadter, Richard, ed. *Great Issues in American History.* Vol. 2, *From the Revolution to the Civil War, 1765–1865.* New York: Random House, Vintage Books, 1958.

Nevins, Allan. *The Emergence of Lincoln.* New York: Charles Scribner's Sons, 1950.

Nevins, Allan. *The Statesmanship of the Civil War.* New York: Macmillan Co., 1962.

Ramsdell, Charles W. "Lincoln and Fort Sumter." *The Journal of Southern History* 3 (1937): 259–288.

Randall, James G. *Lincoln the President.* 4 vols. New York: Dodd, Mead, 1945–1955.

Sandburg, Carl. *Abraham Lincoln: The Prairie Years and the War Years.* New York: Harcourt, Brace & Co., 1954.

Thomas, Benjamin. *Abraham Lincoln*. New York: Alfred
  A. Knopf, 1952.
Van Doren Stern, Phillip. *The Life and Writings of Abra-
  ham Lincoln*. New York: Random House, 1940.

Chapter Five

Blackford, Susan L., and Blackford, Charles M., eds. *Let-
  ters from Lee's Army*. New York: Charles Scribner's
  Sons, 1947.
Carter, Robert Goldthwaite. "Four Brothers in Blue." *The
  Maine Bugle,* 1 October 1898.
Catton, Bruce. *Mr. Lincoln's Army*. New York: Double-
  day, 1968.
Coddington, Edwin B. *The Gettysburg Campaign: A Study
  in Command*. New York: Charles Scribner's Sons, 1968.
Eisenschiml, Otto, and Newman, Ralph. *Eyewitness: The
  Civil War As We Lived It*. New York: Grosset & Dun-
  lap, 1956.
Foote, Shelby. *The Civil War: A Narrative*. 3 vols. New
  York: Random House, 1958–1974.
Fremantle, Arthur J. L., and Haskell, Frank A. *Two
  Views of Gettysburg*. Chicago: R. R. Donnelley & Sons,
  1964.
*Harper's Pictorial History of the Great Rebellion in the
  United States*. New York: Harper & Bros., 1866.
Johns, Henry T. *Life with the Forty-Ninth Massachusetts
  Volunteers*. New York: Ramsey & Bisbee, 1890.
McCarthy, Carlton. *Detailed Minutiae of Soldier Life in
  the Army of Northern Virginia*. New York: J. W. Ran-
  dolph and English, 1888.
Meade, George Gordon. *The Life and Letters of George
  Gordon Meade*. 2 vols. New York: Charles Scribner's
  Sons, 1913.
Miers, Earl Schenck. *Billy Yank and Johnny Reb*. Chi-
  cago: Rand McNally, 1959.
Nevins, Allan. *Ordeal of the Union*. 8 vols. New York:
  Charles Scribner's Sons, 1959–1971.

Nevins, Allan. *The Statesmanship of the Civil War*. New York: Macmillan Co., 1962.

Stevenson, William G. *Thirteen Months in the Rebel Army*. New York: A. S. Barnes and Burr, 1862.

Thomason, John W., Jr. *Jeb Stuart*. New York: Charles Scribner's Sons, 1930.

INDEX

Abolitionism, as cause of Civil War, 27–28; early history in America, 112–113; and American Colonization Society, 113; William Lloyd Garrison and, 113–114; and American Anti-Slavery Society, 114; opposition to, 114; methods of arousing public, 114–115; and political parties, 115; Booth case in Wisconsin, 116–118; historians' interpretations of, 121–123

"A House Divided" speech (Lincoln), 20–21

Alien and Sedition Acts, 10

American Anti-Slavery Society, 114, 121

American Colonization Society, 113

Anderson, Major Robert, in command at Fort Sumter, 134, 135, 136, 137

Armies, recruitment of, 146–153

Army life, 154–158

Barnes, Gilbert, on abolitionism, 121

Battles, Fort Sumter, 130–140; Second Bull Run, 141; Forts Henry and Donelson, 149; Shiloh, 149; Fredericksburg, 158–159; Chancellorsville, 159–160; Brandy Station, 161–162; Gettysburg, 169–193

Beale, Howard K., on causes of Civil War, 13–14

Beard, Charles A., on causes of Civil War, 24–27

Bennett, Lerone, Jr., on early history of slavery in U.S., 84–85

Bidwell, John, to California, 43

Birney, James G., presidential candidate, 115; abolitionist, 121

Blair, Montgomery, and Fort Sumter, 134–135

Booth, Sherman M., abolitionist editor, 116–118

Brandy Station, battle, 161–162, 165

Brooks, Preston S., and Sumner caning, 120

Brown, John, abolitionist, Harper's Ferry raid, 122

Brown, Moses, and first textile mill, 39

Buchanan, James, and homestead act, 25; leadership, 31; and Sherman M. Booth, 118; lack of statesmanship, 125; and Fort Sumter, 132

Buell, Augustus, Union view of Gettysburg, 178–180

Burnside, General Ambrose E., as commander of Army of the Potomac, 158

Calhoun, John C., and southern view of Constitution and Union, 36; early career and War of 1812, 36–37; compared to Webster, 65–66; attitude toward tariff, 66; secretary of war and vice-president, 66; *South Carolina Exposition*, 66; change in political philosophy, 66–67; views on Constitution, 66–67; elected to Senate, 68; and Wilmot Proviso, 68; on Compromise of 1850, 68; historians' view of, 68–70; and limits to slavery expansion, 78

California, 75–77

90–91; alleged benefits of, 91–92; Negro attitudes toward, 94–99; runaway slaves, 99; slave revolts, 99–100; legal codes, 100; blacks as objects, 101; religion among slaves, 101–102; black family life under, 102–105; relations among slaves, 105–108; house slaves, 106–107; black drivers, 107–108; economic aspects of, 108–111; defenders of, 110–111; and abolitionists, 111–123; and Lincoln's use as issue, 141

Slave states, 78

Small farmers, in South, 62–64

Smith, Caleb, and Fort Sumter, 135

Smith, Jedediah, fur trader, 44

Soldier life, in war, 154–158

South, the, Robert E. Lee and, 13–14; and conspiracy theory of Civil War causes, 17–18; attitudes toward tariff and internal improvements, 25; attitudes toward slavery extension and fugitive slave law, 25; and control of federal government, 25–26; attitude toward causes of Civil War, 27–29; as section, 52–71; geography and economy, 52–57; importance of cotton in, 53–57; cities in, 54–56; population mix and class structure, 57–58; social structure, 60; education and cultural life, 60–61; state and local government, 61; small farmers, poor and mountain whites in, 62–65; middle class in, 63–64; desire to control West, 77–78; attitude toward Texas annexation, 78; area and population, 1850, 78; beginning of slavery in, 81–85; slave revolts in, 99–100

South Carolina, nullification controversy, 66–68; and tariff, 1832, 67; and Force Bill, 68; and secession, 132

South Carolina Exposition (Calhoun), 66

Southerners, on causes of Civil War, 17–18, 27–29; and Compromise of 1850, 51, 68; attitude toward cotton, 56–57; desire to own plantations, 59–60; interest in literature and politics, 61; characterized, 62; attitudes toward Union, 65; attitudes toward slavery, 81; reaction to slave revolts, 99–100; attitudes toward abolitionism, 118; in Kansas, 118; and Sumner speech and caning, 118–120; and Fort Sumter, 130–133, 136; Lincoln's attitude toward, 143

Stanton, Edward, secretary of war, 150

Statesmanship, in pre-Civil War period, 125–126

Stephens, Alexander, Confederate vice-president, 132

Stuart, General J.E.B., and Brandy Station, 165–166; described, 166–167; and Gettysburg, 167–171

Sumner, Charles, "Crime Against Kansas" speech, 118–119; caning in Senate, 120

Tappan brothers, abolitionists, 121

Taylor, Zachary, president, 31

Textile mills, New England, beginnings, 39, 40; life in, 42–43; farm girls as mill hands, 43

Thomas, John, on abolitionism, 121–122

Thompson, William T., on Lowell, Mass., 41–42